Crazy
Right Wing Republicans
and
How They Got That Way

CURTIS A. MOORE

DEDICATION

To My Kids, Sarah and Travis, Who Started All This; My Helpmate of 25 Years, Lorraine Giovinazzo; And, Most of All, My Wife, Judy.

ACKNOWLEDGMENTS

There are simply too many people to thank by name.
So many helped, and thank you all. There is one exception: special thanks to Andy Hrycyna, formerly of Beacon Press, who pressed me time and again for an explanation of what happened to America. This is the answer.

CONTENTS

PREFACE

It is difficult to get a man to understand something, when his salary depends on his not understanding it.

Upton Sinclair
I, Candidate for Governor: And How I Got Licked
University of California Press
1994

This book started in 1985 as an attempt to learn more about global warming. It is now ending more than thirty years later with, I believe, the possible death of American freedom at hand, a victim of the ultra-rich, and the Republican party.

That, believe it or not, is true. It does, however, require an explanation. This is it.

In 1985, I had spent two weeks criss-crossing the United States, interviewing scientists from New York City to Irvine, California—a group that later included two Nobel laureates, the president of the U.S. National Academy of Sciences and the president of the American Association for the Advancement of Science. All agreed that global warming was happening, that it was due to human activity and the chances were quite good that a "tipping point" would be reached that would catapult the Earth's climate into something never before experienced—not unlike a nuclear explosion, an avalanche instead of a trickle of snow, or the passing of some invisible point of no return like that which later brought down the Twin Towers on September 11, 2001.

It was my job as counsel to the Republican members of the U.S. Senate Committee on Environment and Public Works to talk with scientists, understand what they concluded and why. As a former reporter for the Associated Press, as well as a lawyer, my skills and intuition were prized, because I could often spot an issue developing years in advance—something that former reporters were uniquely good at.

In addition, I was comfortable with Republicans. My former boss, Sen. William V. Roth, Jr. of Delaware might have gained fame as one of the fathers of "trickle down" economics, but I was most proud of him when he threw General Motors and Chrysler lobbyists out of his office, saying he was an environmentalist.

The Senator at whose will I served in 1985, Robert T. Stafford of Vermont, had guided the state through one of its worst economic crises by tightening its belt, but in the Senate he beat back attempts by Ronald Reagan's appointees to undo protections of the nation's air, water, and soils. He then presided over a thorough house cleaning, which saw all of Reagan appointees to the Environmental Protection Agency, save one, booted out of office.

There was, in short, a very substantial wing of the Republican Party that was not only moderate to liberal, but quite proud of that. It seemed certain that our next great test would be posed by global warming. After that trip, all of my instincts screamed this at me.

But nothing happened. We held hearings, introduced legislation, made statements on the floor of the U.S. Senate, demonstrated that the world was warming, what the consequences would be, and why. Still, nothing happened. In 1989, I left the Committee, puzzled.

In January 1989, I found Washington lobbying or lawyering to be inconsistent with my self-image—how could I spend a career fighting for the environment, then lobby against it for, say, General Motors or DuPont? So I combined a return to my earlier career as a reporter, while eking out a living providing clients with advice on international environmental policies and technologies. They ranged from Greenpeace and the American Lung Association to the Southern California Gas and Tokyo Electric Power Companies.

But the puzzle of why I was unable to predict public response to global warming was seldom far from my mind. The editor of my first book, Andy Hrycyna of Beacon Press, and I would spend hours trying to understand why the United States, which had ignited a global environmental revolution, was creeping steadily to the rear, being passed by the likes of Germany and Japan.

For years, I was baffled by why such a manifest, grave, and urgent threat was being ignored. As the years passed, the case in support of global warming grew steadily, inexorably stronger and stronger, as I knew it would.

But still, there was no action.

Then I discovered the reason:

Starting in about 1972, David and Charles Koch and other rich men and women heeded the advice of corporate lawyer (and soon-to-be U.S. Supreme Court Justice) Lewis Powell's Manifesto to remake America, recasting it into a nation more friendly to the rich and their interests, especially oil. Global warming was not, even then, a trivial threat. Action to prevent it meant the death of fire—oil, coal, and the trillions in profits that they generated being burned in cars, trucks, industrial furnaces, and the mighty electricity-generating behemoths. All would be required to end, because they were too dangerous for human survival.

But ExxonMobil, Chevron, Koch Petroleum, oil producing nations (and states like Oklahoma, Kansas, and Texas), could not allow action to be taken. Instead, they skimmed a tiny fraction of their profits, deployed that money to change America generally, and specifically, set out to destroy environmental science and scientists.

And, in the process, they were remaking America. No longer would it be a land of equal opportunity, but instead one of inherited wealth. No longer would the ultra-rich pay their fair share of taxes, but instead that burden would fall to those of lower income. No longer would it be a democracy, but instead it would become a nation of "neoliberalism"[a] in which government was no longer the solution to the problem, but itself the problem.

The rich, ultra-rich, and Republicans succeeded famously.

I discovered the "Powell Manifesto," written as a call to arms for corporations and the rich by Lewis Powell just before he was appointed to the U.S. Supreme Court by President Richard Nixon. Off the court, corporations implemented the manifesto, founding the Business Roundtable and hiring thousands of lobbyists.

On the Supreme Court, Powell himself implemented the Manifesto, securing a 5-4 decision in which the court held for the first time in 1978's *First National Bank of Boston v. Bellotti* that a corporation had the same right to speech as a human. Roughly 32 years later, *Bellotti* was cited more than 80 times as the court held in the *Citizens United* case that money was speech, so corporations and the rich could spend as much as they wanted in political campaigns, giving birth to superPACs.

---

[a] According to Investopedia, the term "liberal" in economics is different than in politics. Liberalism in economics refers to "freeing up" the economy by removing barriers and restrictions, such as regulations or other controls on what actors can do. Neoliberalism's policies seek to create a *laissez-faire* system.

At about the same time as *Bellotti*, came the clarion call by former Secretary of the Treasury and energy czar, William Simon, for a takeover of the Republican Party—without which it was doomed, he wrote, to become the "stupid party" and die. Quickly, a raft of state and national level so-called "think tanks" like the Heritage Foundation and the Cato Institute were founded, respectively by beer magnate Joe Coors and oil billionaires Charles and David Koch.

What Simon called a "counterintelligensia" was created. The Kochs developed and put in place systems to identify, school, and place bright young teenagers. Hundreds of state-level counterparts to the federal think tanks were created and funded. Foundations to do all of this were established, and because tax payers had to make up for the revenue shortfall created by deducting contributions to these so-called "charities," even ordinary citizens helped pay for all this.

Gradually, the Republican Party began shifting toward the interests of the rich, and away from ordinary people. Barry Goldwater ran an overtly racist campaign, capturing his home state of Arizona and five of the deep south. Nixon, realizing that if Goldwater could advocate the use of nuclear weapons by field commanders and still carry six states, a candidate who appeared reasonable could easily carry the nation—and he did in 1968 and 1972.

The Republican Party reached out to religious fundamentalists, with one of its operatives, Paul Weyrich, coining the phrase "moral majority". Other segments were recruited by appeals to "values" such as opposition to abortion and to gay rights. But the judges appointed were almost invariably corporate lawyers like Lewis Powell, as well as Chief Justices John Roberts and William Rhenquist.

Nixon resigned in scandal, but the GOP continued shifting toward the rich. Reagan fought Ford for the Presidential nomination in 1976, lost, but won it and the Presidency in 1980. From that point on, it was off to the races.

What followed were years of consolidation and, for those who believed in global warming, defeat. President Bill Clinton's tax on energy, which was principally to slow global warming, suffered a crushing defeat when a single oil-state Senator, Democrat David Boren of Oklahoma, was manipulated by the Koch brothers and ExxonMobil, to kill it.

It took until about 2010 to piece this all together, then two more to write a book about it. That was *Cliffs I: How and Why America's Billionaires and the Republican/Libertarian/Tea Party Are Pushing Us Over*. It is the predicate for this book. *Cliffs I* explained what had happened, because I knew that absent such an explanation, nobody would believe the terrible hoax that has been played on the world.

But *Cliffs I* was written and printed after the U.S. Supreme Court's decision equating money with speech in the 2010 *Citizens United* case. I scoffed at the time, not believing that money could play a bigger role than it already was—after all, when a member of Congress could legally buy himself a car and tune-up, another could pay for his son's move to Washington, D.C., and yet a third fly Miss Michigan to Washington, D.C. to testify before his own Committee, how could money possibly come to play an even bigger role?

Boy, was I wrong.

The nation's ultra-rich, the top one-tenth of one percent in wealth and income, seized the opportunity presented by *Citizens United*. They completed transformation of the Republican Party into the "liberty" party, so its role advancing the interests of the rich and their corporations is virtually complete. Republicans have won in 2010, 2012 (except for the presidency), and 2014, and are now poised for yet another victory. All that remains to complete it is the election of 2016.

Republicans have turned into a party of crazy, right wing allies of the rich and their corporations. The election of 2016 may be—I am convinced that it is—our last chance to save ourselves.

1

CRAZY RIGHT WING REPUBLICANS AND HOW THEY GOT THAT WAY

Aided by massive sums of money from the ultra-rich, like the two Koch brothers, who are richer than 133 of the world's nations, the Republican Party has moved further and further to the right since the 2012 elections.

These are not your grandfather's Republicans. They are the most pro-corporation and pro-rich ever elected in the United States, committed not only to the wealthy, but to policies favored by them: drastic cuts in federal spending and taxes, transformation of Medicare and Medicaid into private voucher programs, changing Social Security so stock markets will make money from it, and abolition of the corporate, estate, and the alternative minimum taxes, all embodied in the budget proposed by the nation's senior Republican, House Speaker Paul Ryan of Wisconsin.[1]

He and other modern Republicans would cut $5 trillion in spending over a decade, with major cuts in programs for the poor, including Medicaid and food stamps. They have voted at least 37 times to repeal "Obamacare" health insurance, formally known as the Affordable Care Act,[2] and called for major—and unrequested by the armed services—increases in military spending, while cutting nearly all other discretionary domestic programs.[3]

All that stands between these men and women and virtually complete control of the United States is a single election, and they have committed to spending $889 million—twice what Mitt Romney spent in 2012—on it. So far, fewer than 400 families have contributed nearly half the money raised in the 2016 presidential campaign, with roughly 130 families and their businesses providing more than half the money that Republican candidates and their superPACs had raised through June 2015.[4]

- Republicans control the House and Senate for the first time in eight years. They will have their largest House majority in more than 75 years.[5]

- Republicans now control 31 governorships, which the Washington Post calls "near a high water mark in the modern era."[6]

- Republicans now control 29 state legislatures, holding both chambers—the most since the 1920s.[7]

- Republicans are a majority of attorneys general, 27, compared to 23 for Democrats.[a, 8] In each state, the attorney general is not only chief legal advisor to the state government, but also the state's chief law enforcement officer.

- They control the U.S. Supreme Court when it suits them, and through it have opened the floodgates to unlimited "independent" campaign spending to secure the chokehold of the rich and their corporations on the United States.[9]

The U.S. Supreme Court's January 2010 holding in *Citizens United* that money is speech, enables corporations and the rich to spend as much as they want, so multi-billionaires have become the kings of American politics. They have seized control of primaries, using them to litmus test candidates as Americans for Prosperity (AFP) does, by requiring Republican candidates to sign a No Climate Tax Pledge, which its president, Tom Phillips, says is aimed not only at preventing action on global warming, but also barring expansion of solar, wind and other forms of renewable energy.[b]

"What it means for candidates on the Republican side is, if you … buy into green energy or you play footsie on this issue, you do so at your political peril," Phillips told *National Journal* magazine.[10]

---

[a] Douglas Chin, an independent, was appointed Attorney General of Hawaii by Gov. David Yutaka Ige, a Democrat.

[b] AFP's "Hot Air Tour," a national tour that calls predictions of global warming "hysteria," labels cap and trade legislation a "climate tax," and features a hot air balloon is one such stunt. AFP also runs the website No Climate Tax, which exhorts citizens to send a message to federal and state lawmakers urging them to sign the No Climate Tax Pledge. Other astroturf organizations conceived by Phillips under the AFP banner include: "Free Our Energy," a group promoting increased domestic drilling.

Phillips himself concedes that the argument is not about science, saying "I'm not a scientist and don't pretend to be." It is, he said, a matter of his ideology, which he describes as "a free-market ideology that says lower taxes, less government spending, less government regulation is a better way to economic prosperity and that the government cannot create prosperity."[11]

Today's Republicans bear no resemblance to those who founded the Party expressly to halt the spread of slavery, and were forced to end it altogether. To preserve a unified nation, they fought a war they didn't start—the bloodiest in U.S. history.

There would be no United States today were it not for those Republicans—but America's billionaires have seized control of the nation, wresting it from moderates and the middle class. Aided by a sympathetic U.S. Supreme Court that has confused money with words, and conferred the right of speech, including the giving of unlimited amounts of money, on the nation's billionaires.

None has done more to alter the American system of government than Charles and David Koch, especially when combined with the other billionaires they've recruited. Perhaps no organization commands more deference in Republican politics nowadays than the sprawling operation established by these multi-billionaire brothers, ranked by *Forbes* magazine as tied as the sixth richest people in the world with a net worth of $42.9 billion each.[12]

Charles and David Koch are by no means the only sources of money. Sheldon Adelson makes billions running Las Vegas Sands, America's largest casino company, and he uses that money to buy influence in the Republican Party. Nothing illustrates the GOP godfather's reach better than the so-called Adelson Primary: In 2014, candidates such as Jeb Bush, John Kasich and Chris Christie flew to Vegas to meet with Adelson, detail their visions and, they hoped, receive his blessing and his money.[13]

Warren Buffet, with a net worth of $62.9 billion, is richer than even the Kochs,[14] but he doesn't give his money away to politicians. In 2014, Buffett made 15 campaign contributions totaling $120,400.[15] "I just don't believe that the elections should be decided by the super-rich," he said. Being a billionaire, he has said, shouldn't mean he can "outshout everybody else."[16]

Tom Steyer, a California billionaire, termed an "environmental crusader" by the Sunlight Foundation, had never contributed to a superPAC before March 2013, but has given $70 million since, supposedly making him the largest single contributor to superPACs of all time, until 2014.[17] Steyer, however, gives to Democrats.

What the Kochs and many of the other ultra-rich have done, however, is give money in large sums and consistently, spanning not a few years, but decades. Some money has gone to politicians, but other contributions fund universities and think tanks, scholarships and advanced placements with right wing politicians and agencies. The Kochs made their first investment at least as early as 1974, and before they started, their father, Fred, was a charter member of the viciously anti-Communist John Birch Society.

Although the twice-a-year seminars hosted by the Kochs have attracted the most attention is the past decade, they have been in the business consistently and for a long time. Others may have boosted the fortunes of a specific candidate or cause, but the Kochs and a relatively small number of other ultra-rich have changed America.

Since the floodgates were opened by the Powell Manifesto, money poured in vast sums from the few wealthy families and individuals, which has remade America. These ultra-rich, including the Kochs, Scaifes, Bradleys, and DeVos family of Michigan, "were among a small, rarefied group of hugely wealthy, archconservative families that for decades poured money, often with little public disclosure, into influencing how the Americans thought and voted," the book says.[18]

As soul mates in what they considered a war over American values, the groups to which he gave shared a core set of conservative beliefs, evident in the way they described their missions.

For example, the Foundation for Economic Education promotes "individual freedom, private property, limited government, free trade." The Pacific Legal Foundation works "for less government and the preservation of free enterprise, private property rights and individual liberties." The Reason Foundation advocates "public policies based upon individual liberty and responsibility and a free-market approach." Lower taxes and fewer regulations are also part of the broadly shared program.[19]

Fueled since 2003 by money and commitments collected at twice-a-year, Koch-sponsored seminars at posh resorts, their premise is simple: get people to stop giving money to schools, museums, and hospitals—even to Republican organizations, such as the Party itself or one of its arms. Instead, "start giving money to things that will save the country."[20]

Assuming a total net wealth of $100 billion,[21] the Koch's riches are so great that only 60 nations, starting with Morocco's GDP of $103,836 billion, are richer than the Kochs.[22]

Now they are owners of a vast empire with products ranging from Brawny paper towels, Dixie cups, Georgia-Pacific lumber, Stainmaster carpet, Lycra, and Koch gasoline, which the Kochs started in 1967 with a stake of $356 million inherited from their father, Fred, who started the company he left them, Rock Island Oil & Refining.[a] While not an oil company to rival, say, ExxonMobil, they control at least four oil refineries, six ethanol plants, a natural, gas-fired power plant, and 4,000 miles of pipeline.[23]

The brothers' embrace of libertarian, right-wing politics seems to have begun in 1974, when Charles and others founded the Charles Koch Foundation (renamed the Cato Institute in 1976), a libertarian think tank headquartered in Washington, D.C.[24] In 1978, Charles conceded in an article for *Reason* magazine that he and David had "a radical philosophy."[25] Then they demonstrated the truth of the statement when, in 1980, David ran for Vice President as the Libertarian Party nominee. He supported legalization of abortion and repeal of criminal penalties for drug use, prostitution, and homosexuality.

In an echo of what was to come later, David attacked campaign donation limits, while the Libertarian Party wanted to eliminate the FBI and the CIA, federal regulatory agencies, such as the Securities and Exchange Commission and the Department of Energy, abolish Social Security, minimum-wage laws, gun control, and all personal and corporate income taxes.[26]

Does this sound familiar? *It should, because except for abolishing the CIA and FBI this is precisely what today's Republicans demand—and the rich do, too.*

---

[a] What the Koch brothers inherited from their father, Fred, was a company worth over $356 million in 2015 dollars. When Fred Koch died in 1967, Rock Island Oil & Refining (which would become Koch Industries) had recurring earnings the year before of about $4 million and a net worth of approximately $50 million. The company had 1,200 employees. (KochFacts.com, http://www.kochfacts.com/kf/misrepresentations-about-koch-family-and-koch-industries-history/, accessed Nov. 13, 2015.) According to one site used for calculating the value of money over time, (DollarTimes, http://www.dollartimes.com/calculators/inflation.htm, accessed Nov. 12, 2015) $50,000,000.00 in 1967 had the same buying power as $356,857,142.86 in 2015. Annual inflation over this period was 4.18 percent.

We know this because in 2010–11, a group of researchers based at Northwestern University published findings from the country's first-ever representative survey of the richest one percent of Americans. The study, known as the Survey of Economically Successful Americans and the Common Good, canvassed a random sample of 104 representatives from Chicago-area households, with a median wealth of $7.5 million. Those canvassed were granted anonymity to discuss their views candidly.[27]

Their replies were striking. Most members of the one percent were concerned about the common good—but their beliefs about how to achieve "the common good" differ markedly from ordinary citizens.

Right wing Republicans, not Democrats. Where merely affluent Americans are more likely to identify as Democrats than as Republicans, the ultrawealthy overwhelmingly leaned right.

Less Government. The one percent emphasize relying on free markets or private philanthropy to produce good outcomes, thinking in terms of "getting government out of the way" to solve public problems.

Likely to Give to Politicians—and Access Them. They are far more likely to raise money for politicians and to have access to them; nearly half had personally contacted one of Illinois's two United States senators, and about half of the one percent contacted an official at least once in the last six months.

Oppose a Higher Minimum Wage. Where the general public overwhelmingly supports a high minimum wage, the one percent were broadly opposed.

Oppose Safety Net. A majority of Americans supported expanding safety-net and retirement programs, while most of the very wealthy supported cutting, rather than expanding popular entitlement programs, such as Social Security and Medicare.

Charter schools and "profitizing" government. Most of the one percent favored charter schools, merit pay, and other market-oriented education reforms. More than two-thirds say the federal government "has gone too far in regulating business and free enterprise."

Taxes. From 1950 to 1980, the incomes of the top earning one-tenth of one percent of Americans rose 80 percent. Since the election of Ronald Reagan in 1980 and the adoption of "supply side" economics, the income of the top one-tenth of one percent has risen 403 percent.[28] That's because most wage increases are going to those at the top, not those in the middle. Americans are not enthusiastic about higher taxes generally, but they do feel strongly that the rich should pay more than they do.

Deficit. More members of the one percent point to the federal budget deficit as the country's most pressing problem than to any other problem facing the nation. In contrast, only five percent of the general public believe the deficit is the nation's most serious problem. Instead, 57 percent were more concerned about the economy and jobs.

"Probably the biggest single area of disconnect has to do with social welfare programs," said Benjamin I. Page, a political scientist at Northwestern University and a co-author of the study. "The other big area has to do with paying for those programs, particularly taxes on high-income and wealthy people."

Many states and the federal government are a case study of the disconnect between what average citizens want the government to do, and what it does. One of the authors later wrote a paper describing the results, and said the following:

(E)conomic elites and organized groups representing business interests have substantial independent impacts on U.S. government policy, while mass-based interest groups and average citizens have little or no independent influence.[29]

In 1980, when the American public was provided with a choice to embrace this platform, most (50.75 percent) voted for Ronald Reagan, a large number (41.01 percent) for Jimmy Carter, a few (6.61 percent) for John Anderson, but only 1.06 percent, fewer than one million, for what is today favored by the rich and their Republicans.[30]

But it has been more than 35 years since that Presidential election of 1980, and if Charles and David are anything, they are patient, determined, even tenacious, men. They have quietly persevered, and won.

CHAPTER 1 ENDNOTES

1. David M. Herszenhorn, "Devotion to Fiscal Policy May Keep Ryan From Taking House Speaker's Job," *New York Times*, Oct. 14, 2015.

2. Stephanie Condon, "House GOP votes to repeal Obamacare, again," May 16, 2013, CBS News, http://www.cbsnews.com/news/house-gop-votes-to-repeal-obamacare-again/, accessed Dec. 15, 2015.

3. David M. Herszenhorn, "Devotion to Fiscal Policy May Keep Ryan From Taking House Speaker's Job," *New York Times*, Oct. 14, 2015.

4. Ashley Parker, "Donald Trump Attacks as Republican Rivals Court Donors at Koch Retreat," *New York Times*, Aug. 2, 2015.

5. "How will Washington change with Republican Congress in 2015?" CBS News, Jan. 1, 2015, http://www.cbsnews.com/news/how-will-washington-change-with-republican-congress-in-2015/, accessed Nov. 6, 2015.

6. Reid Wilson, "Republican sweep extends to state level," *Washington Post*, Nov. 5, 2014.

7. "Even worse news for Democrats: Republicans triumph at state level, too," *The Economist*, Nov. 4, 2014.

8. Ballotpedia, http://ballotpedia.org/Attorney_General#2015, accessed Nov. 6, 2015.

9. Fredreka Schouten, "Koch brothers set $889 million budget for 2016," *USA TODAY*, Jan. 27, 2015.

10. Jason M. Breslow, "Tim Phillips: The Case Against Climate Legislation," Frontline, PBS, Oct. 23, 2012, http://www.pbs.org/wgbh/frontline/article/tim-phillips-the-case-against-climate-legislation/, accessed Dec. 15, 2015.

11. Jason M. Breslow, "Tim Phillips: The Case Against Climate Legislation," Frontline, PBS, Oct. 23, 2012, http://www.pbs.org/wgbh/frontline/article/tim-phillips-the-case-against-climate-legislation/, accessed Dec. 15, 2015.

12. "The World's Billionaires," *Forbes*, http://www.forbes.com/billionaires/, accessed Dec. 16, 2015.

13. Forbes 400, " #15 Sheldon Adelson," *Forbes*, http://www.forbes.com/profile/sheldon-adelson/, accessed Dec. 18, 2015.

14. Forbes, "The World's Most Powerful People: #13 Warren Buffett," http://www.forbes.com/profile/warren-buffett/, accessed Dec. 18, 2015.

15. Campaign Money,com,
http://www.campaignmoney.com/political/contributions/warren-buffett.asp?cycle=16,
accessed Dec. 18, 2015.

16. Chris Isidore and Poppy Harlow, "Buffett: I won't give millions to candidates,"
CNNMoney April 3, 2015,
http://money.cnn.com/2015/04/02/news/companies/buffett-hillary-donation/index.html,
accessed Dec. 18, 2015.

17. Peter Olsen-Phillips, "Revenge of the Democrats: Wealthy liberals top list of super PAC
donors in 2014," Sunlight Foundation,
http://sunlightfoundation.com/blog/2014/10/24/revenge-of-the-democrats/, Oct. 24, 2014,
accessed Dec. 18, 2015.

18. Nicholas Confessore, "Father of Koch Brothers Helped Build Nazi Oil Refinery, Book
Says," *New York Times*, Jan. 11, 2016.

19. Robert G. Kaiser and Ira Chinoy, "Scaife: Funding Father of the Right," *Washington
Post*, May 2., 1999

20. Kenneth P. Vogel, *Big Money: 2.5 billion dollars, one suspicious vehicle and a
pimp—on the trail of the ultra-rich hijacking American politics*, PublicAffairs Books, New
York, 2014.

21. Ashley Alman, "Koch Brothers Net Worth Soars Past $100 Billion, *The Huffington Post,*
April 16, 2014.Ashley Alman

22. "GDP and its breakdown at current prices in US Dollars," United Nations Statistics
Division, December 2014, accessed Dec. 1, 2015.

23. Tim Dickinson, "Inside the Koch Brothers' Toxic Empire," *Rolling Stone*, Sep. 24, 2014,
http://www.rollingstone.com/politics/news/inside-the-koch-brothers-toxic-empire-20140924#
ixzz3uazx8rjQ, accessed Nov. 14, 2015.

24. Why the name "Cato" was chosen is unclear. The Koch brothers have said it was
"envisioned as a committed force to advance free societies" (Allen McDuffee, "Koch
brothers vs. Cato: Charles Koch Institute e-mails alumni," *Washington Post*, March 7, 2012)
A more likely reason is because Cato the Elder fervently opposed what he saw as the
moral decline of Rome. It was suffering from economic decline and inflation, plagues, food
shortages and invasions—both militarily and immigration—and an indifference to the plight
of the state. (Answers.com, "What are the moral reasons for the fall of Rome?"
http://www.answers.com/Q/What_are_
the_moral_reasons_for_the_fall_of_rome, accessed Dec. 17, 2015.)

25. Brian Doherty, "David Koch Ran for Vice President with the Libertarian Party in 1980.
The New York Times Thinks You Should Care, Isn't Sure Why." *Reason*,
https://reason.com/blog/2014/05/19/david-koch-ran-for-vice-president-with-t, May. 19, 2014,
7:31 pm, accessed Dec. 17, 2015.

26. Nicholas Confessore, "Quixotic '80 Campaign Gave Birth to Kochs' Powerful Network," *New York Times*, May 17, 2014.

27. Page BI, Bartels LM, Seawright J. Democracy and the policy preferences of wealthy Americans. *Perspectives on Politics*. 2013 Mar 1;11(01):51–73.

28. David Cay Johnston, "9 Things The Rich Don't Want You To Know About Taxes," *Willamette Weekly,* April 12, 2011.

29. Gilens M, Page BI. Testing theories of American politics: Elites, interest groups, and average citizens. *Perspectives on politics.* 2014 Sep 1;12(03):564–81.

30. "1980 Presidential General Election Results," http://uselectionatlas.org/RESULTS/national.php?year=1980, accessed Dec. 17, 2015.

2
MONEY

Let's start first with the source of power: money. Each of the Koch brothers, Charles and David, have more of it than any other person on the planet, save five. If all their money were attributed to one or the other, he would be the single richest person alive.[a]

Together, they and their allies dominate politics in the United States. But rising gaps in wealth and income are global phenomena, according to the charity Oxfam, which calculated that in 2015, just 62 individuals had the same wealth as 3.6 billion people. This number had shrunk 84 percent, since 2010 where it was 388 individuals.[1]

During the same time that the wealth of the world's 62 richest people rose more than half a trillion dollars, or about 44 percent, that of the bottom half fell by just over a trillion dollars, or about a 41 percent drop. The daily income of the world's poorest 10 percent has risen by less than a single cent every year.[2]

In the United States, there are several streams of money, all with common sources. In no particular order, there are the foundations, with either a finite source of money (from the amount donated when the charity was created) or an on-going, potentially infinite source (from the continuing profits of, say, Koch Industries, Foster Friess' Brandywine Fund, John Schnatter's Papa John's pizza chain, Carl Berg's real estate holdings, Ken Griffin's hedge fund, Citadel, John W. Childs' private-equity investments or sales of Fred Klipsch's speakers, all of whom have given vast sums to take over American democracy).[b]

---

[a] Forbes, "The World's Billionaires," 2015 Ranking, http://www.forbes.com/billionaires/, accessed Dec. 25, 2015.

[b] In the case of the Koch brothers, it is generated by a company worth about $100 billion, and the brothers are, according to *Forbes* magazine, worth about $90 billion. That's about $600 for

(continued...)

11

These millionaires, billionaires, and foundations support hundreds of other organizations. Some are at the state level and are members of the State Policy Network (see Appendix A for a list of them). Others are at the national level, many headquartered in the District of Columbia or its suburbs. Many have familiar names, such as the Cato Institute and the Heritage Foundation, while others are more obscure, such as Accuracy In Media and the Prometheus Institute.

The foundations are coordinated by the Philanthropy Roundtable, a nonprofit with a mission "to foster excellence in philanthropy, to protect philanthropic freedom, to assist donors in achieving their philanthropic intent, and to help donors advance liberty, opportunity, and personal responsibility in America and abroad."[3] It was started in 1987 as a right-wing alternative to the mainstream Council on Foundations, which has 1,750 members.[4]

Then there is a political stream of money.[a] It flows to political action committees (PACs) and, increasingly, to superPACs. Each candidate has one or more superPACs.

For example, Right to Rise is the superPAC supporting Jeb Bush's campaign,[5] while Keep the Promise, a constellation of four superPACs, is backing Ted Cruz.[6]

By the letter of the law, as stated in the U.S. Supreme Court's decision in *Citizens United*, these superPACs are supposedly independent of candidates, and their spending is uncoordinated with candidates. The reality is probably very different.

For example, the superPAC, Take America Back PAC, is supporting former U.S. Sen. Rick Santorum, and is being run by Santorum's former campaign

---

[b] (...continued)
every man, woman and child in the United States. Foster Fries data from Sourcewatch, http://www.sourcewatch.org/index.php/Foster_Friess, Art Pope data from Wikipedia, https://en.wikipedia.org/wiki/Art_Pope; John Schnatter, Carl Berg, Ken Griffin, John W. Childs, Fred Klipsch data from http://www.motherjones.com/politics/2014/02/koch-brothers-palm-springs-donor-list, all accessed Dec. 25, 2015.

[a] In fairness, neither the Kochs nor their allies are the top *political* donors. That honor belongs to institutions and organizations, like the Service Employees International Union, which tops a list compiled by OpenSecrets of the Center for Responsive Politics, at $224,273,550. (Though even individual human beings can hide behind organizations: OpenSecrets says the number five campaign contributor is the Las Vegas Sands, which is owned and controlled by Seldon Adelson, who gave $30,950 to liberals, compared $70,379,411, or 99.95 percent, conservatives/Republicans. Center for Responsive Politics, OpenSecrets.org, "Top Organization Contributors," http://www.opensecrets.org/orgs/list.php, accessed Dec. 19, 2015.

manager and two other staff members who left his campaign, they say, to support him on their own.[7]

Like Charles and David, their allies are also multi-billionaires. Perhaps not as rich as the Kochs, but wealthy beyond the wildest imaginings of ordinary humans.

[The following describes the operation of the Koch foundations, but simply strike Koch and substitute another—say the "John William Pope" or the "Richard and Helen DeVos" or the "Lynde and Harry Bradley" or any one of about 336 foundations identified by Conservative Transparency.[8]]

The Koch brothers own the nation's second largest family-owned company, which means that they are not bothered by the burdens of publicly-held corporations, like ExxonMobil, General Motors or DuPont. Owning the company outright, David and Charles do pretty much as they please, whenever they wish.

Several foundations are used to distribute much of the money. If one or more of the foundations runs low on funds, David or Charles simply pay themselves, then transfer the money to a foundation. They operate six Koch-led private foundations serving somewhat different purposes. (See Box.)

On top of all this, Charles and David can give as they see fit. Each makes over $43 million a day.

THE KOCH FOUNDATIONS

- The Charles Koch Foundation, the primary vehicle for funding colleges and universities.
- The Fred C. and Mary R. Koch Foundation, named for their parents, which focuses much, but by no means all, of its spending on schools and arts organizations in Kansas.
- David H. Koch Charitable Foundation, which focuses on the arts, especially in and around New York City, where David lives.
- The Claude R. Lambe Charitable Foundation, which generally funds conservative think tanks, though it was shut down in 2013.
- The Knowledge and Progress Fund, of which Charles Koch is chairman. In 2012, it made a lone $800,000 grant for "general operating support" to Donors Trust, a tax-exempt, Virginia-based charity that, in accordance with Charles' instructions, funds pro-free market think tanks throughout the nation.
- The relatively small Koch Cultural Trust, which received almost all of its $164,000 in 2012 revenue from funds transferred to it by the Fred C. and Mary R. Koch Foundation. It provides students from Kansas with grants in music, dance, theater, art or screen writing.
- The Charles Koch Institute, a nonprofit that spent $8.57 million during 2012 to fund hundreds of internships, fellowships and associate placements.

Of course, you and I contribute as well, though we do not know it.

The vast majority of the Koch donations are to so-called charities, so they can be deducted, much like gifts that you or I make to churches or the Salvation Army. Making up for that lost tax income falls to you and me, so, like it or not, we're helping to pay for first class air fare for judges to attend seminars in Montana or the publication of *Reason* magazine, including the current issue which boasts articles about Sens. Ted Cruz, Marco Rubio, Jeb Bush, Donald Trump and House Speaker Paul Ryan.

Then there's the money that Charles and David can raise with their twice-a-year seminars at posh resorts, attended by like-minded millionaires and billionaires—and that's a lot, all destined for campaigns.

The Kochs have said that before Barrack Obama became President, not many gave heavily at the twice-a-year seminars. That changed with his election, and the basic model of the Koch operation, starting in 2008, was that cash flowed from the donors who attended twice-a-year summits.[9]

By the 2008–09 elections, Koch retreats—the first in which Democrat and African American Barrack Obama was President—began attracting those who wrote checks in the millions with little hesitation. America's richest—almost all men—began to pledge immense sums, and by the time the conference broke up, the Kochs had salted away $49 million.[10]

The results in 2010 were unarguable. Republicans rode the Tea Party to victory in 2010, taking Iowa, Idaho, Alaska, Wisconsin and Ohio. Provoked by initiatives targeting unions, Democrats and angry activists recalled Wisconsin governor Scott Walker. The Kochs rushed to his defense, filling the air with pro-Walker advertisements saying voters should "Stand with Walker". The Kochs, and Wisconsin voters, did.

* * *

Those attending the Koch seminars are unlike you and me. They are overwhelmingly white, rich, older and male, in a nation that is being remade by the young, by women, and by black and brown voters. Although the United States is vast and sprawls from the Atlantic Ocean to the Pacific, the attendees live in closed communities of wealth. Their neighborhoods are exclusive, and usually gated, dotting a handful of cities and towns. And in an economy that has minted billionaires in a dizzying array of industries, most made their fortunes in just two: finance and energy.[11]

More than a dozen donors or members of their families have been involved with the seminars hosted by the Kochs. They include Doug Deason, a Dallas investor whose family put $5 million behind the Presidential run Gov. Rick Perry of Texas before he dropped out; the brokerage pioneer Charles Schwab, whose wife, Helen, is among the donors; and Karen Buchwald Wright, whose family company makes compressors used to extract and transport natural gas.[12]

Deason wrote a letter to the *Dallas Morning News* in February 2015, defending the Koch brothers and complaining that "We're in the midst of the slowest economic recovery in over 50 years. The labor participation rate is at its lowest level since 1978, when Jimmy Carter was president. Families are making less today than they did six years ago. For the first time in recorded history, more businesses are now dying than starting."[13]

Like many of the advertisements run by superPACs, Deason's letter was a tissue of lies and half-truths.

"Most of the people at the Koch seminars are entrepreneurs who have built it from the ground up—they built it themselves," said Deason, elsewhere.[14] Yes a few are.[a]

But Doug Deason is not. He is the son of Darwin Deason, who *is* self-made and worth $1.38 billion, according to *Forbes* Magazine.[15, 16]

Others who signed the Deason's letter included Thomas Ollis "Tom" Hicks, Sr., and his son, Thomas, who is a "junior". Hicks Senior, is now worth $1 billion according to *Forbes* magazine, and is himself son of a Texas radio station owner.[17] He is a former owner of the Texas Rangers, the Dallas Stars, and the Mesquite Championship Rodeo. Are either Tom Hicks Sr. or Tom Hicks Jr. "Entrepreneurs who have built it from the ground up?" No. Senior, like the Kochs, inherited his start, and Junior will no doubt get something like $1 billion, making him one of only 536 Americans.[18]

---

[a] Kenneth Gerard Langone, Sr., for example, was born Sept. 16, 1935, and is today worth $3.1 billion according to *Forbes* and is best known for co-founding The Home Depot. There is no doubt that Langone is a self-made man. The second of two sons, he was born in Roslyn Heights on Long Island, New York. Neither of his parents, who were the children of Italian immigrants, attended school beyond junior high. Ken's father worked as a plumber and his mother worked in the cafeteria at the small public school across the street from their house.

Too often the positions taken by the top one percent, or the top one-tenth of one percent, are based on facts that are either untrue, or taken completely out of context.

Let's examine some of those claims from Deason's 2015 letter to the Dallas Morning News—which Deason, undoubtedly believes.

This is the "slowest economic recovery in 50 years." Is this the same economy that Dun & Bradstreet described in January 2015: "payment delinquency and business failure risks declined for the month among all U.S. businesses. All told, signs of improvement on Main Street support D&B's cautiously optimistic view for economic growth in 2015."[19]

What of the labor participation rate, which he said "was at its lowest since 1978." True—but the labor participation rate was *even lower* from 1948 to 1978, during the presidencies of Dwight Eisenhower, Richard Nixon and Gerald Ford (as well as, of course, Harry Truman, John Kennedy and Lyndon Johnson).[20]

Is it true, as Deason claims, that "families are making less today than they did six years ago"? Yes, it's true that household income was lower in February 2015 than six years earlier. *But that decline started when George W. Bush entered office*, dropping sharply in his last year, 2008. More importantly, *household income under Barrack Obama is higher in 2014 dollars than it was when Ronald Reagan was President.*[21]

E. PIERCE MARSHALL, FOREST HOGLUND AND LEE ROY MITCHELL

Other signers included E. Pierce Marshall Jr., whose father's fortune was valued at $1.7 billion by *Forbes,*[22] and whose grandfather, also a billionaire, married Anna Nicole Smith, *Playboy* magazine's 1993 Playmate of the Year.[23] Also signing was Forrest Hoglund, President of SeaOne Maritime Corp., which transports natural gas, who was President of Enron Oil & Gas Company from May 1990 to December 1996.[24] Another signer, Lee Roy Mitchell, heads the Cinemark chain of movies and "grew up around his family's theatre business."[25]

Make no mistake, those attending the seminars are a *Who's Who* of billionaires, and also include the following:

ART POPE

One, for example, is Art Pope, who inherited money from his father John William Pope, who founded Variety Wholesalers, the largest privately-owned, retail variety store chain in the southeast. John's wealth was boosted in 1949, when he assumed control of his father's five discount-variety stores in Fuquay Springs, N.C.[26]

Pope and his family own a department store chain known throughout the southeast, Roses, which caters to low-income buyers, especially African Americans. It is the wholly-owned subsidiary of Variety Wholesalers, which operates a number of chains that are household names in the south, all catering to low-income customers. They include 52 Eagle stores, 54 McCrory/United stores, 118 Value Mart stores, 145 Super Dollar stores, 53 P.H. Rose stores, 106 Allied stores, 33 Maxway stores, 60 Bargain Town stores,106 Roses stores, and 118 Bonus Stores/Bill's Dollar Stores.[27] In 2010, the John William Pope Foundation, run by Rose's heir, Art Pope, gave Americans for Prosperity $1.25 million.[28]

After the *Citizens United* decision freed them of campaign giving restraints, Pope and his family donated more than $500,000 to state candidates and party committees in 2010 and 2012, according to an analysis of state campaign finance data by the Institute for Southern Studies, a liberal research group. His company, Variety Wholesalers, gave almost $1 million more to outside groups that ran independent campaigns.[29]

PHIL ANSCHUTZ

Another Koch supporter, Phil Anschutz,[30] was also born to wealth. After buying his father's drilling company, Circle A Drilling, in 1961, Anschutz bought ranches in Colorado, Utah and Wyoming, and eventually went into the oil-drilling business. Phil's grandfather, Carl, was an ethnic German who emigrated from Russia and started the Farmers State Bank in Russell, Kansas.[31]

Ranked by *Forbes* as the 38th richest person in the U.S., with an estimated net worth of $11 billion as of 2014,[32] Anschutz bought the 250,000-acre Baughman Farms, one of the country's largest farming corporations, in Liberal, Kansas for $10 million in 1970. The following year, he acquired nine million acres along the Utah-Wyoming border. This produced his first fortune in the oil business.[33]

In the early 1980s, the Anschutz Ranch, with its one billion barrel oil pocket, became the largest oil field discovery in the United States since Prudhoe Bay in Alaska in 1968. He sold an interest in it to Mobil Oil for $500 million in 1982.[34]

Over four decades Anschutz has built fortunes from oilfields (Anschutz Exploration Co.), railroads (Southern Pacific), telecom (Qwest Communications), sports teams (Los Angeles Kings and a third of the Lakers), movie making (The Chronicles of Narnia), and, most recently, concerts and arenas (AEG).[35]

Anschutz buys access: At the bottom of a typewritten letter thanking the billionaire for a $100,000 contribution, Jim Nicholson, then the Republican National Committee chairman, scrawled: "I hope your meeting with Trent Lott was productive. Thanks Phil!"[36]

But Anschutz's ownership of the *Washington Examiner*, a daily tabloid, and the *Weekly Standard*, probably the nation's most influential conservative magazine, has given him a megaphone for his right-wing views on taxes, national security, and President Barack Obama, which the 130 or so companies he owns have not provided him.[37]

STANLEY HUBBARD

Stanley Hubbard's family company Hubbard Broadcasting donated $150,000 in 2014 to Freedom Partners Action Fund.[38] His father, Stanley Eugene Hubbard, founded Hubbard Broadcasting.[39] According to Forbes magazine, his net worth is $2.1 billion

PAUL SINGER

Paul Singer, a billionaire New York investor, in a signal victory for Marco Rubio, is supporting him in his race for the Republican presidential nomination.[40]

According to Forbes, Singer's net worth is $2.1 billion, mostly from "the large, and growing, hedge fund Elliott Management," which he founded and today has $27 billion under management.[41]

Singer gave more money to Republican candidates and causes in 2014 than any donor in the country, according to the Center for Responsive Politics. He is courted by Republicans both for the depth of his own pockets and for his wide network of other conservative givers. He is known for his caution and careful vetting of candidates.[42]

According to the *New York Times*, the battle for Singer's support included months of behind-the-scenes lobbying by aides and appearances by candidates over the last year at dinners and breakfasts convened by him. It, said the *Times*, "underscores the growing clout of big donors in presidential elections, particularly this year, when 'superPACs,' and the wealthy donors who finance them, have moved to the center of the race."[43]

The *Times* describes Singer as an assiduous and effective "bundler" for candidates, who in 2012 not only raised more than $3 million to elect Mitt Romney, the eventual Republican nominee, but who provides strategic guidance to other donors in the New York financial world.

See Appendix C for a list of those thanked at a 2011 seminar for given $1 million or more.

LIMITED GOVERNMENT, LIMITED SPENDING AND FREE ENTERPRISE

In truth, the giving at the Koch seminars and elsewhere reflects the political stakes for the families and businesses that have moved most aggressively to take advantage of *Citizens United*, particularly in the energy and finance industries. Many donations were made from business addresses or post office boxes, or wound through limited liability corporations or trusts, exploiting the new avenues opened up by *Citizens United*, which gave corporate entities far more leeway to spend money on behalf of candidates, so long as the expenditures were "independent" of them.[44]

The families investing the most in presidential politics overwhelmingly lean right, contributing tens of millions of dollars to support Republican candidates who have pledged to pare regulations; cut taxes on income, capital gains and inheritances; and shrink entitlement programs.[45]

A review of what is supported and what is opposed by a variety of groups—the Club for Growth, for example—provides a revealing list of anti-government policies.

The Club for Growth describes itself as a—

national network of over 100,000 pro-growth, limited government Americans who share in the belief that prosperity and opportunity come from economic freedom. The leading free-enterprise advocacy group in the nation, we win tough battles and we have an enormous influence on economic policy.[46]

Mallory Factor, a businessman who started a rival group, the Free Enterprise Fund, explained, "This country was built on competition," adding that "The only people who get threatened by competition are the ones without new ideas," who, instead of building a better mousetrap, "have lawyers and the government shut down the other guy's mousetrap."[47]

The Club harbors a pathological fear of government—not just big government, but any government whatsoever. Export-Import Bank? Opposed. "No Child Left Behind" minimum standards for educating students? Opposed. National health insurance? Opposed.

But what of measures to privatize or "profitize" government responsibility? The Club for Growth supports those. School vouchers? Support. Personal retirement accounts? Support. Profitize Social Security? Support.

Limited spending and limited government are the mantra of not only the Club for Growth, but for Americans for Prosperity, FreedomWorks, Tea Party Patriots, the libertarian Cato Institute, the Heritage Foundation. Indeed, Michael A. Needham, the leader of Heritage Action for America, is telling House Republicans that it is time for "moving away from the U.S. Chamber of Commerce's preferred agenda."[48]

Charles Koch describes himself as a "classical liberal," saying that "gains in productivity have dropped, the gains in income for the middle class and the least advantaged have slowed," and he is seeking candidates who will reverse these trends.[49] The Koch brothers and their allies are true revolutionaries, intent on upending the system entirely and severing ties between Republicans and the corporate and business interests that have long nurtured them.

In that respect, the Kochs and their allies are further implementing the conversion of the Republican Party into the "Liberty Party," advocated by William Simon, the Secretary of the Treasury and energy "czar" of the Nixon and Ford Administrations.[a]

Charles Koch did, in fact, meet in a session described as follows—

Charles Koch's views are based on his extensive study of the theory and practice of social cooperation for mutual gain—and prosperous societies. His verdict for private property, free markets, and the rule of law—and against government intervention—is long

---

[a] See the "Counterintelligensia" chapter of my book, *Cliffs I: How and Why America's Billionaires and the Republican/Libertarian/Tea Party Are Pushing Us Over.*

held. An incident back in the 1970s regarding federal energy policy and Koch Industries is illustrative.

> William Simon, the top energy regulator in the Nixon's Federal Energy Administration, received oil company head after head in his office demanding this or that to alleviate their oil shortage. Many wanted to receive more entitlements credit for their refineries. But Koch Industries had come by to just ask the federal government to leave them alone—to allow price signals to allocate crude oil and petroleum products. It was a meeting that Simon and his office would not forget.[50, a]

In his 1977 book, *A Time to Choose*, Simon advocated the creation of a "counterintelligensia" based on universities and a wide variety of free market "think tanks." Simon did his best to see that effort become a reality as head of the Olin Foundation, but it was Charles and David Koch that turned his dream into fact.

Another representative of the new libertarian wing of the Republican Party is former U.S. Sen. Jim DeMint, a South Carolina Republican. He sought to replace No Child Left Behind with a state-based, block-grant program for schools. DeMint also worked to privatize Social Security by allowing the creation of individual investment accounts in the federal program. In 2003, DeMint sponsored legislation to allow people under the age of 55 to set aside three to eight percent of their Social Security withholding income in personal investment accounts.[51]

In 2013, DeMint left the Senate to become head of the Heritage Foundation, founded by Paul Weyrich, with money from Joseph Coors, who was "stirred" by Lewis Powell's Manifesto. DeMint heads not only Heritage, but its political arm, Heritage Foundation America, which was founded in 2010 as the Tea Party protests were gaining strength.

The rise of the Tea Party libertarians has driven a sharp wedge between those who form the party's right flank today, and the corporate and business advocates who were once its embodiment.

---

[a] The author who is the source for this information, Robert L. Bradley Jr., is now with the Institute for Energy Research (IER), founded in 1989 from a predecessor non-profit organization registered by Charles G. Koch and Robert L. Bradley Jr. It advocates positions on environmental issues including deregulation of utilities, climate change denial, and claims that conventional energy sources are virtually limitless. SourceWatch, http://www.sourcewatch.org/index.php?title=Institute_for_Energy_Research, accessed Dec. 26, 2015.

Jack Kemp, a conservative hero who (together with my former boss, the late Sen. William V. Roth, Jr. of Delaware) proposed a tax cut to fund Ronald Reagan's theory of "trickle down" economics, saw promise in the partnership of business and government. Kemp believed that promoting business-friendly policies was good for the nation and the Republican party. That was when the source of most money was the business community. But those days are over.

Today, the term Chamber of Commerce Republican is an insult hurled by hard-right activists who savage "crony capitalism," saying that "When big business and big government get together, we are all sunk" in the words of Adam Brandon, the chief executive of FreedomWorks.[52]

The rise of the Tea Party and other libertarian forces has driven a wedge in the Republican Party, dividing the business advocates and corporate interests that have traditionally been its base, from those who are opposed to government in all its forms.

The two Heritage groups, FreedomWorks, some Tea Party organizations and the Club for Growth, while virtually unknown outside Washington, form a coalition of hardline conservative groups fighting to seize control of the Republican agenda.[53]

The rich are a small group that have channeled money into suffocating political power. They have seized the advantage bestowed by *Citizens United*, to make secret donations that create new, and supposedly independent superPACs. They have exercised the authority of *Bellotti* to insert corporation "speech" into the thicket of politics. They have exploited the loophole of money-is-speech created by *Buckley v. Valeo* to promise a 2016 campaign fund of $889 million, almost twice what the GOP Republican nominee Mitt Romney spent.

The rich have created new organizations—Americans for Prosperity, FreedomWorks, and the various tea party groups—to mobilize armies of paid staff at the national and state levels. They have interposed themselves in arguments at the city level over road funding, in school boards over charter schools, and at the state levels over union power. They have carved new paths for infusing money into campaigns.

"Economic winners in an age of rising inequality," wrote the *New York Times*, "operating largely out of public view, they are reshaping government with fortunes so large as to defy the ordinary financial scale of politics." Midway through the presidential race of 2016, a *New York Times* analysis found in

November 2015 that up to that point, just 158 families had provided nearly half of the early campaign money.

By the author's reckoning, about one-third of the Koch supporters come from the world of finance, another one-third from oil, gas, coal or other fossil fuel interests, and a final one-third from a variety of other fields. They pretend to be first generation entrepreneurs (and some are), but most are living on, and increasing, second and third generation inherited wealth.

Those people don't think like the average American, even the average rich American. They see no need for a liveable minimum wage, a safety net of social security, Medicare and Medicaid for those cast adrift by the fates, or taxes on their wealth to assure that they pay their fair share.

Almost all are Republican, though there is a smattering of Democrats. But to a remarkable degree, their philosophies are becoming part of a widely adopted blueprint for public officials around the country: critical of the power of unions, many are also determined to reduce spending and taxation, and are skeptical of government-led efforts to mitigate the growing gap between the rich and everyone else.

They have rejected the historical involvement of the wealthy in good works, building libraries, lavishing wealth on universities, or helping those less fortunate. Never before, even in the time of railroad barons and industrial tycoons, have the rich employed money to further their own selfish interests, and to impose their will on the entire nation, whether it likes it or not.

CHAPTER 2 ENDNOTES

1. Oxfam, *An Economy For The 1%*,
https://www.oxfam.org/sites/www.oxfam.org/files/file_attachments/bp210-economy-one-per
cent-tax-havens-180116-en_0.pdf, accessed Jan. 19, 2016.

2. Oxfam, *An Economy For The 1%*,
https://www.oxfam.org/sites/www.oxfam.org/files/file_attachments/bp210-economy-one-per
cent-tax-havens-180116-en_0.pdf, accessed Jan. 19, 2016.

3. Philanthropy Roundtable, "Guiding Principles, Mission, Offerings,"
http://www.philanthropyroundtable.org/, accessed Dec. 19, 2015.

4. Wikipedia, "Philanthropy Roundtable,"
https://en.wikipedia.org/wiki/Philanthropy_Roundtable and "Council on Foundations,"
https://en.wikipedia.org/wiki/Council_on_Foundations, both accessed Dec. 19, 2015.

5. Nick Corasaniti, "'Super PAC' Supporting Jeb Bush Attacks Donald Trump in New Ad,"
New York Times, Dec. 17, 2015.

6. Theodore Schleifer, "First on CNN: Ted Cruz Super PACs target Oklahoma, Missouri,
Kansas," Cable Network News, Dec.15, 2015.

7. Ben Gittleson and Shushannah Walshe, "Rick Santorum Staffers Switch Tactics, Form
Super PAC," ABC News, August 6, 2015.

8. Conservative Transparency, http://conservativetransparency.org/donors/, accessed Jan.
19, 2016.

9. Kenneth P. Vogel, *Big Money: 2.5 billion dollars, one suspicious vehicle and a pimp—on
the trail of the ultra-rich hijacking American politics*, PublicAffairs Books, New York, 2014.

10. Daniel Schulman, *Sons of Wichita*, Grand Central Publishing, New York, 2014.

11. Nicholas Confessore, Sarah ,Cohen and Karen Yourish, "From Only 158 Families, Half
the Cash for '16 Race," *New York Times*, Oct. 10, 2015.

12. Nicholas Confessore, Sarah ,Cohen and Karen Yourish, "From Only 158 Families, Half
the Cash for '16 Race," *New York Times*, Oct. 10, 2015.

13. Holly and Doug Deason, " Holly and Doug Deason: What do the Koch brothers want?
To defend the American dream," *Dallas Morning News*, Feb. 2, 2015.

14. Nicholas Confessore, Sarah Cohen, and Karen Yourish, "From Only 158 Families, Half
the Cash for '16 Race," *New York Times*, Oct. 10, 2015.

15. "Darwin Deason contributes $7.75 million to fund Cyber Security Institute, Innovation
Gym," Jan. 30, 2014, http://www.smu.edu/SecondCentury/News/2014/DarwinDeasonGift,
accessed Nov. 30, 2015.

16. http://www.forbes.com/profile/darwin-deason/, *Forbes* magazine, accessed Nov. 30, 2015.

17. Wikipedia, https://en.wikipedia.org/wiki/Tom_Hicks, accessed Nov. 30, 2015.

18. Wikipedia, https://en.wikipedia.org/wiki/List_of_countries_by_the_number_of_US_dollar_billionaires#North_America, accessed Dec. 25, 2015.

19. Dun & Bradstreet, http://www.dnb.com/lc/credit-education/us-business-economic-trends-2015-02.html, accessed Nov. 30, 2015.

20. FactCheck.org, Robert Farley, "Declining Labor Participation Rates," March 11, 2015, http://www.factcheck.org/2015/03/declining-labor-participation-rates/, accessed Nov. 30, 2015.

21. U.S. Bureau of the Census, "Income and Poverty in the United States, 2014," https://www.census.gov/content/dam/Census/library/publications/2015/demo/p60-252.pdf, accessed Nov. 30, 2015.

22. "Forbes 400 List for 2005," http://forbes.com, May 2005.

23. Wikipedia, https://en.wikipedia.org/wiki/E._Pierce_Marshall#cite_ref-7, accessed Nov. 30, 2015.

24. Bloomberg Business, http://www.bloomberg.com/research/stocks/private/person.asp?personId=1133823&privcapId=41865656, accessed Nov. 30, 2015.

25. http://www.businesswire.com/news/home/20111116006218/en/Lee-Roy-Mitchell-Founder-Cinemark-USA-Named, accessed Nov. 30, 2015.

26. John William Pope Foundation, "About John William Pope," https://jwpf.org/about/about-john-william-pope/, accessed Nov. 18, 2015.

27. Variety Wholesalers, "About Variety Wholesalers," http://www.vwstores.com/page/show/id/6528, accessed Nov. 18, 2015.

28. Foundation Center, http://990s.foundationcenter.org/990pf_pdf_archive/581/581691765/581691765_201106_990PF.pdf?_ga=1.112167748.1324181612.1446146040, accessed Nov. 18, 2015.

29. Matea Gold, "In N.C., conservative donor Art Pope sits at heart of government he helped transform," *Washington Post*, July 19, 2014.

30. Dealbook, "Secretive G.O.P. Donors Are Planning Ahead," Oct. 20, 2010, http://dealbook.nytimes.com/2010/10/20/secretive-republican-donors-are-planning-ahead/?_r=0, accessed Nov. 20, 2015.

31. Wikipedia, Philip Anschutz, https://en.wikipedia.org/wiki/Philip_Anschutz, accessed Nov. 20, 2015.

32. *Forbes* topic page on Philip Anschutz, accessed Nov. 20, 2015.

33. Wikipedia, Philip Anschutz, https://en.wikipedia.org/wiki/Philip_Anschutz, accessed Nov. 20, 2015.

34. Wikipedia, Philip Anschutz, https://en.wikipedia.org/wiki/Philip_Anschutz, accessed Nov. 20, 2015.

35. *Forbes*, "Phil Anschutz," http://www.forbes.com/profile/philip-anschutz/, accessed Nov. 20, 2015.

36. Adam Cohen, "Editorial Observer; Buying a High-Priced Upgrade on the Political Back-Scratching Circuit," *New York Times,* Sep. 15, 2003.

37. Michael Calderone, "Phil Anschutz's conservative agenda," *Politico,* http://www.politico.com/story/2009/10/phil-anschutzs-conservative-agenda-028355, accessed Nov. 20, 2015.

38. Brian Lambert, "Stanley Hubbard is a major contributor to Koch brothers' new super PAC," *MinnPost*, Oct. 15, 2014, https://www.minnpost.com/glean/2014/10/stanley-hubbard-major-contributor-koch-brothers-new-super-pac, accessed Nov. 20, 2015.

39. Wikipedia, "Stanley Hubbard," https://en.wikipedia.org/wiki/Stanley_Hubbard, accessed Nov. 20, 2015.

40. Maggie Haberman and Nicholas Confessore, "Paul Singer, Influential Billionaire, Throws Support to Marco Rubio for President," *New York Times*, Oct. 30, 2015.

41. *Forbes magazine,* "Paul Singer," http://www.forbes.com/profile/paul-singer/,, accessed Nov. 23, 2015.

42. Maggie Haberman and Nicholas Confessore, "Paul Singer, Influential Billionaire, Throws Support to Marco Rubio for President," *New York Times*, Oct. 30, 2015.

43. Maggie Haberman and Nicholas Confessore, "Paul Singer, Influential Billionaire, Throws Support to Marco Rubio for President," *New York Times*, Oct. 30, 2015.

44. Nicholas Confessore, Sarah Cohen and Karen Yourish, "From Only 158 Families, Half the Cash for '16 Race," *New York Times*, Oct. 10, 2015.

45. Nicholas Confessore, Sarah Cohen and Karen Yourish, "From Only 158 Families, Half the Cash for '16 Race," *New York Times*, Oct. 10, 2015.

46. The Club for Growth, http://www.clubforgrowth.org/, accessed Dec. 25, 2015.

47. David D. Kirkpatrick, "Leadership Dispute Causes a Split in a Powerhouse of Fund-Raising for Conservative Causes," *New York Times,* July 8, 2005.

48. David D. Kirkpatrick, "Leadership Dispute Causes a Split in a Powerhouse of Fund-Raising for Conservative Causes," *New York Times,* July 8, 2005.

49. Matea Gold, "Charles Koch on the 2016 race, climate change and whether he has too much power," *Washington Post*, August 4, 2015.

50. Robert Bradley Jr., "Charles Koch on Cronyism (Part 1)," Oct. 27, 2015, https://www.masterresource.org/ckoch/charles-koch-vs-cronyism-I/, accessed Dec. 26, 2015. Bradley writes that the source of this information was a former colleague of Simon's: "This anecdote was told to me by William A. Johnson, Simon's number two at the Federal Energy Administration."

51. Wikipedia, Jim DeMint, https://en.wikipedia.org/wiki/Jim_DeMint#cite_ref-1, accessed Nov. 24, 2015.

52. Carl Hulse, "Paul Ryan Lands at Center of a Rivalry for the Soul of the G.O.P.," *New York Times*, Nov. 2, 2015.

53. Philip Elliott and Steve Peoples, "Conservative Groups Driving GOP Agenda," Associated Press, Nov. 1, 2013.

3

IT'S HAPPENING EVERYWHERE, AND IT'S ALL ABOUT MONEY

The ultra-rich have seized power in state capitols, and to maintain it have created funds to divert rivers of cash into campaign accounts. Increasingly, the rich have run for office themselves, contributing millions to their own campaigns, breaking records.

Eye-popping sums continue to flow after the elections, bleeding from politics into governing. Election results, bought with cash, affirmed an agenda of shrinking government, taxes and regulation. New governors and mayors proposed tort "reform," barring citizens from courts. They created "right-to-work zones," in which union membership and dues would be voluntary; and a half-dozen constitutional amendments.

In many states, however, including old union strongholds of the Midwest like Indiana and Ohio, the rising distrust in government voiced by the rich and their corporations has proved a more powerful force in mobilizing voters—particularly with enough money behind it. Here are stories from individual states.

"EMERGENCY MANAGEMENT" IN MICHIGAN POISONS WATER

In Michigan, within months of being elected governor, Republican Rick Snyder pushed a series of signature tax reforms through the Legislature in 2011.

Snyder's plans relied heavily on the premise that lower taxes for businesses would create a stellar turnaround, ending the depression that gripped the state when he took office.

But four years later, a close analysis by the *Detroit Free Press* of tax incomes showed that the cost of funding state government had shifted to those who can least afford it, and the job growth that might have justified that shift had not materialized.[1]

For some Michigan families, changes to tax credits and deductions were being deeply felt. The state was collecting nearly $900 million a year more from individuals, many of them poor people who had lost tax credits or deductions. Meanwhile, businesses paid about $1.7 billion less in taxes, all while job growth has slowed each year since the tax cuts took effect.[2]

Snyder also signed into law another bill passed by the Republican legislature, which was also, literally, a disaster. It authorized him to declare a "financial emergency" in towns or school districts. An emergency manager could then fire local elected officials, break contracts, seize and sell assets, eliminate services, and even eliminate whole cities or school districts without any public input.[3]

In Pontiac, a city about 60 miles north of Detroit, Emergency Manager Louis Schimmel came very close: he cut Pontiac's budget almost in half, consolidated 87 different benefit plans for employees into one single coverage option, created a regional fire department with neighboring Waterford Township (and shuttering Pontiac's), and eliminated the police force in favor of a contract for Oakland County to patrol the city.[4]

In November 2012, Michigan voters repealed the law. Within six weeks Republican legislators passed a new version.[5]

In Flint, a state-appointed emergency manager, Darnell Early, increased property taxes, utility rates by 25 percent, cut the city's workforce by 20 percent, reduced employee compensation by 20 percent, eliminated retiree healthcare for new employees, and slashed services to residents and visitors.[6] Then in April 2014, he switched the city water source from unpolluted Lake Huron to the long-polluted and corrosive Flint River in a bid to save money.[7]

By January, Flint residents were up in arms. Hundreds turned out to meet a powerless mayor and City Council. Flint resident Qiana Dawson said her four-year-old and two-year-old had broken out in rashes, while LeeAnne Walters said her three-year-old, with a compromised immune system, suffered skin problems after bathing.[8]

They pressed for a return to Lake Huron/Detroit River water, Earley said that was so cost prohibitive that Flint "can ill-afford to switch course."[9]

For one year, Flint citizens complained of the taste, odor and appearance of the chocolate-colored water coming from their taps, but were largely ignored by state officials. The state also dismissed reports of elevated lead levels in the blood of Flint children from pediatrician Dr. Mona Hanna-Attisha, before for the first time publicly acknowledging a problem in October 2015. Still, it was January 14, 2016 before Michigan's Gov. Snyder asked President Obama to provide emergency water supplies.[10]

THE RICHEST MAN IN ILLINOIS

On a warm spring day in 2013, Kenneth C. Griffin, the billionaire founder of one of the world's largest hedge funds, rose before a black-tie dinner of the Economic Club of Chicago to deliver an urgent plea to the city's elite.[11]

Politicians spent too much and drove businesses and jobs from the state. They had refused to help those who would take on the reigning powers in the Illinois Capitol. "It is time for us to do something," he implored.

Their response came quickly. In the months since, Griffin and a small group of rich supporters—not just from Chicago, but also from New York City, Los Angeles, southern Florida, and Texas—have poured tens of millions of dollars into the state, a concentration of political money without precedent in Illinois history.[12]

Their wealth forcefully shifted the state's balance of power. In 2014, the families helped elect as governor, Bruce Rauner, a Griffin friend and former private equity executive from the Chicago suburbs, who estimated his own fortune at more than $500 million. Then, they rallied behind Rauner's agenda: to cut spending and overhaul the state's pension system, impose term limits and weaken public employee unions.[13]

As in many other states, to encourage Republican lawmakers to stick with him on tough votes, the governor contributed hundreds of thousands of dollars to them. Ex-aides set up a superPAC designed to support state lawmakers who back a pre-conceived agenda and oppose those who stand in the way. In the case of Illinois, the group's main contributor was a financier and Republican donor, who gave $4 million.[14]

Illinois, and the tax cuts in Michigan, are representative of what has happened at other state levels.

NORTH CAROLINA: BUYING A STATE

According to the *New Yorker* magazine, "Republican politics in North Carolina are characterized by a tight interweaving of elected officials with think tanks and advocacy groups."[15]

At the center is Art Pope, head of a privately-owned company that owns one of the southern Mid Atlantic's largest department store chains, Roses, which he inherited from his father. Pope also heads the non-profit, John William Pope Center for Higher Education Policy, founded by him and named for his father.

Art Pope donated almost a quarter of a million dollars in support of North Carolina Republican candidates in the 2010 election, and groups with close ties to him gave more than $2 million to them.[16]

In 2012, after Pope and his companies gave a reported $450,000 toward the Republican takeover of the governorship and the state legislature, he co-chaired Gov. McCrory's transition team, then was the state's budget director.[17] (Pope, has also been a board member of Americans for Prosperity, and is a regular participant in Koch "seminars".)

A Pope Center report urges the adoption in North Carolina of programs dedicated to "the morality of capitalism". Found at 62 public and private colleges and universities, these programs were funded over the past fifteen years by the North Carolina-based BB&T Bank, under its former president John Allison. He was C.E.O. of the Cato Institute, founded by the Koch brothers. In a 2012 statement, Allison explained that the programs "retake the universities" from "statist/collectivist ideas."[18]

ARIZONA: RUNNING A STATE BY THE CENTER FOR ARIZONA POLICY

Since it was established in 1995, Center for Arizona Policy 123, measures supported by it have been signed into law, including the state's 2008 constitutional amendment banning same-sex marriage. That effort was spearheaded by the group's president, Cathi Herrod. Twenty-nine bills backed by CAP have been vetoed by various Arizona governors after being passed by the state legislature.[19]

INDIANA: PROFITIZING WELFARE

One of Mitch Daniels' initial acts as governor was to privatize—that is, to convert it into a profit stream—the administration of the state's welfare support system. He awarded a $1.34 billion contract to IBM to manage the state's welfare system. This taxpayer giveaway met with little resistance, and culminated in disastrous results, with IBM eventually suing the state of Indiana when Daniels rescinded the contract.[20]

Indiana also enacted one of the first voter-ID laws in the nation, despite the fact that studies had shown that voter fraud in the state was negligible and unworthy of legislative resources and attention.[21]

NATIONAL PROFITIZATION

Meanwhile, at the national level, the effects of profitization are immense.

National Defense. By 2008, for example, the U.S. Department of Defense employed 155,826 private contractors in Iraq—and 152,275 troops. "This degree of privatization is unprecedented in modern warfare," wrote the *Christian Science Monitor*.[22]

Prisons. The same has happened to, of all things, prisons. Today, nearly 10 percent of U.S. prisons and jails—translating to 200,000 prisoners—have been turned into profit streams. The three largest companies, CCA, Wackenhut Corrections Corporation, and Cornell Corrections, Inc., have amassed large political influence through government ties, lobbying power, and campaign contributions, while attempting to convert the discourse of justice into the language of the marketplace. They accuse government agencies as having a monopoly on corrections, and espouse the need to downsize and cut through red tape, claiming that they can run prisons more efficiently and cheaper, doing a better job and saving money.[23]

Security Clearances. The company contracted to provide background checks for security clearances for U.S. employees in sensitive positions, but failed to provide adequate information in at least 665,000 instances.[24]

Toll roads. During 2007, sixteen states had some privatized road projects formally proposed or underway. Indiana and Chicago signed multi-billion dollar private concession deals for public roads for 75 years and 99 years, respectively, causing toll rates to increase steadily.[25] In Virginia, officials agreed to spend slightly more than $580 million on the Hampton Roads toll tunnel—more than twice the investment from the companies behind the deal. With no competition, the companies won the right to collect billions of dollars in tolls over 58 years.[26]

Whether manifested in profitization by creating streams of income from the performance of services historically reserved to the government, or the emphasis on limited government and reliance on the market, the United States is being changed faster and more dramatically than at any time in its history. And it's all because of money—and greed.

CHAPTER 3 ENDNOTES

1. Stephen Henderson and Kristi Tanner, "Michigan taxes: Businesses pay less, you pay more," *Detroit Free Press,* Oct. 4, 2014.

2. Stephen Henderson and Kristi Tanner, "Michigan taxes: Businesses pay less, you pay more," *Detroit Free Press,* Oct. 4, 2014.

3. Paul Egan, "Is emergency manager law to blame for Flint water crisis?" *Detroit Free Press*, Oct. 25, 2015.

4. Ashley Woods, "Pontiac Emergency Manager Order Postpones Democracy For City After Financial Crisis," *Huffington Post*, Sep. 17, 2013.

5. Ashley Woods, "Pontiac Emergency Manager Order Postpones Democracy For City After Financial Crisis," *Huffington Post*, Sep. 17, 2013.

6. Darnell Earley, "Guest view of Darnell Earley: Flint bankruptcy an option if retirees' health care lawsuit succeeds," *Flint Journal*, Jan. 24, 2014.

7. "Emergency for Democracy: Unelected Manager Who Caused Flint Water Crisis Now Runs Detroit Schools," *Democracy Now*, Jan. 15, 2016.

8. "Residents share complaints about Flint's water quality," *Detroit News*, Jan. 14, 2015.

9. "Residents share complaints about Flint's water quality," *Detroit News*, Jan. 14, 2015.

10. Paul Egan and Todd Spangler, "President Obama declares emergency in Flint," *Detroit Free Press,* Jan. 16, 2016.

11. Nicholas Confessore, "A Wealthy Governor and His Friends Are Remaking Illinois," *New York Times*, Nov. 29, 2015.

12. Nicholas Confessore, "A Wealthy Governor and His Friends Are Remaking Illinois," *New York Times*, Nov. 29, 2015.

13. Nicholas Confessore, "A Wealthy Governor and His Friends Are Remaking Illinois," *New York Times*, Nov. 29, 2015.

14. Nicholas Confessore, "A Wealthy Governor and His Friends Are Remaking Illinois," *New York Times*, Nov. 29, 2015.

15. Jedediah Purdy, "Ayn Rand Comes to U.N.C.," *New Yorker,* March 19, 2015.

16. Jedediah Purdy, "Ayn Rand Comes to U.N.C.," *New Yorker,* March 19, 2015.

17. Jedediah Purdy, "Ayn Rand Comes to U.N.C.," *New Yorker,* March 19, 2015.

18. Jedediah Purdy, "Ayn Rand Comes to U.N.C.," *New Yorker,* March 19, 2015.

19. Shadee Ashtari, "How One Right-Wing Christian Group Is Leading Arizona's March Toward Conservative Extremism," *The Huffington Post*, Feb. 28. 2014

20. Bryan K. Bullock, "The Ultra-Right-Wing State Nobody Mentions," *Truthout,* June 27, 2014, http://www.truth-out.org/opinion/item/24552-the-ultra-right-wing-state-nobody-mentions, accessed Dec. 19, 2015.

21. Bryan K. Bullock, "The Ultra-Right-Wing State Nobody Mentions," *Truthout,* June 27, 2014, http://www.truth-out.org/opinion/item/24552-the-ultra-right-wing-state-nobody-mentions, accessed Dec. 19, 2015.

22. Molly Dunigan, "A lesson from Iraq war: How to outsource war to private contractors," *Christian Science Monitor*, March 19, 2013.

23. Corrections, "Prison Privatization," http://www.correctionsproject.com/corrections/pris_priv.htm, accessed Dec. 19, 2015.

24. Joe Schneider, "Security Firm Sued by U.S. Over Bad Background Checks," *BloombergBusiness*, Jan. 23, 2014.

25. U.S. PIRG, "Report: 21st Century Transportation Transparent & Accountable Budgets," Sep. 6, 2007.

26. Michael Laris, "Agreement for new submerged tunnel in Norfolk leaves Virginia underwater," *Washington Post*, Oct. 17, 2015.

4
REDISTRICTING, CITIZENS UNITED, AND VICTORY

A majority of Americans disapprove of the Republicans in Congress, according to *Bloomberg Business*, yet it has an edge. Why? Because as a result of the 2010 elections, boundaries are drawn so carefully, that the only votes that often matter come from fellow Republicans.[1]

In the 2010 elections, Republicans won the majority in the U.S. House of Representatives and, more importantly, gained more than 700 state legislative seats across the nation. This gave Republicans control of redistricting, the once-a-decade redrawing of congressional seats. "The advantage," concluded *Bloomberg Business*, "helped them design safer partisan districts and maintain their House majority in 2012."[2]

Republicans lost the presidential race in 2012 to a victorious Barrack Obama, by about 5 million votes. But nationwide, Democratic House candidates combined to win about 1.4 million more votes than Republicans, according to data compiled by *Bloomberg News*.[3]

But that didn't help the Democrats. They lost in 2010, again in 2012—except for the Presidency—again in 2014, and they're headed in the same direction in 2016.

That year, 2010, was also the first election of the Tea Party, which was aided mightily by money from the Koch brothers and their allies, and fueled by the campaigns of FreedomWorks and Americans for Prosperity. The river of money that aided Republicans and the various tea party groups was made possible, of course, by the Republican U.S. Supreme Court in *Citizens United*.

Again, I will emphasize that these are not your grandfather's Republicans, or your father's, or even mine. These men and women bear no resemblance to those who founded the Republican Party or made it great. They have been created out of whole cloth by the rich of America.

This kind of manipulation, called gerrymandering, creates districts that are skewed and uncompetitive. Without question, politicians of every stripe, Democrats as well as Republicans, have gerrymandered. But never before has there been an attempt to take over the entire nation by denying voters the ability to elect representatives who fairly reflect their views.

In the United States, district maps must be redrawn every 10 years, because the Constitution requires a census, and after that there is a redistricting process. State legislators manipulate redistricting to gain advantage for either Democrats or Republicans.

But never before has there been a calculated, richly-funded effort to capture control of elections at the state level and, with them, to redistrict a party into the minority. This is not theoretical: precisely such a thing happened in 2010–2012 with the congressional delegations of Pennsylvania and North Carolina, and to a lesser degree, Arizona.

Are these three states the exception? No.

In 2012, voters in Wisconsin definitely leaned Democratic, voting to re-elect President Obama, choosing Tammy Baldwin to be their new United States senator, and casting more total votes for Democrats than Republicans in the races for Congress and the State Legislature. But because of the redistricting map drawn by Republicans, the GOP outnumbers Democrats in Wisconsin's new Congressional delegation five to three—and controls both houses of the Legislature.[4]

It happened also in Pennsylvania. Obama was re-elected, and Democrats cast about 83,000 more votes for Democratic Congressional candidates than for Republicans. But new maps drawn by Republicans helped ensure that Republicans would have a 13-to-5 majority in the Congressional delegation that the state sent to Washington.[5]

The same happened elsewhere. Democratic Congressional candidates won nearly half the votes in Virginia, but only 27 percent of its seats. In Ohio, Democrats attracted 48 percent of the vote, but won only a quarter of its seats.[6]

These elections demonstrate the control that the rich, and their Republican allies, have established over the entire nation. They suddenly and surprisingly won the 2010 elections, which they then used to consolidate their hold on power.

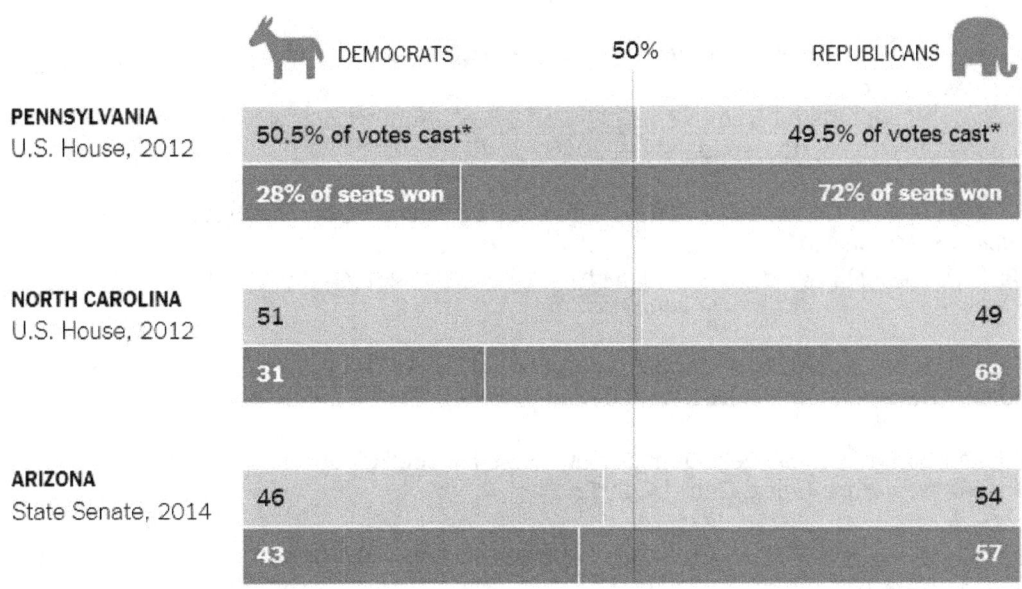

Figures include only votes for Republicans and Democrats, not for other parties.
Source: Sam Wang, Princeton University
By The *New York Times*,
http://www.nytimes.com/2015/12/06/opinion/sunday/let-math-save-our-democracy.html?_r=0

CHAPTER 4 ENDNOTES

1. Greg Giroux, "Republicans Win Congress as Democrats Get Most Votes," *Bloomberg Business*, March 18, 2013, http://www.bloomberg.com/news/articles/2013-03-19/republicans-win-congress-as-democrats-get-most-votes, accessed Jan. 9, 2016.

2. Greg Giroux, "Republicans Win Congress as Democrats Get Most Votes," *Bloomberg Business*, March 18, 2013, http://www.bloomberg.com/news/articles/2013-03-19/republicans-win-congress-as-democrats-get-most-votes, accessed Jan. 9, 2016.

3. Greg Giroux, "Republicans Win Congress as Democrats Get Most Votes," *Bloomberg Business*, March 18, 2013, http://www.bloomberg.com/news/articles/2013-03-19/republicans-win-congress-as-democrats-get-most-votes, accessed Jan. 9, 2016.

4. Griff Palmer and Michael Cooper, "How Maps Helped Republicans Keep an Edge in the House," *New York Times*, Dec. 14, 2012.

5. Griff Palmer and Michael Cooper, "How Maps Helped Republicans Keep an Edge in the House," *New York Times*, Dec. 14, 2012.

6. Griff Palmer and Michael Cooper, "How Maps Helped Republicans Keep an Edge in the House," *New York Times*, Dec. 14, 2012.

5

TOOLS

The rich and ultra-rich have every tool you could wish for. They are all figurative, of course, but to drive a nail, there is a hammer; to cut a board, there's a saw; or to make a hole, there's a drill.

The rich and ultra-rich are not in the business of building a house, so they have no need for a hammer, saw, or drill. Still, to get what they're after—a new and different America, one that operates as they think it should—requires a set of tools, one for sculpting politics and politicians, another for winning the hearts and minds of their donors, and yet a third for planting seeds of philosophy in the minds of the young. They have all these, and many more. In forty or more years, they have become very skilled at using them.

Describing the extent of the vast network of spending is extraordinarily difficult. The first record of its start is 1972, when Colorado brewing magnate Joe Coors was inspired by the Powell Manifesto to give $250,000 to start the Heritage Foundation.[1] Then in 1974, Charles created the Charles G. Koch Foundation (renamed the Cato Institute two years later). He was about 39 at the time, and more than 40 years have passed. During that time, the rich and ultra-rich have been carefully, systematically, and single-mindedly expanding their reach.

The most dangerous of the pro-rich, pro-corporation lot was Lewis Powell, who started this revolution with the Powell Manifesto on August 23, 1971,[a] then proceeded to implement it after joining the U.S. Supreme Court on January 7, 1972.[b]

---

[a] Some scholars trace the rise since 1970 and the subsequent dominance of neoliberalism—the doctrine that market exchange is an ethic in itself, capable of acting as a guide for all human action—to Powell's Manifesto in 1971. See David Harvey, *A Brief History of Neoliberalism,* (Oxford University Press, 2005).

[b] The 5-4 decision that Powell wrote in *First National Bank of Boston v. Bellotti* shifted the direction of First Amendment law by declaring that corporate financial influence

(continued...)

But make no mistake about it: through their immense wealth, the Koch brothers and like-minded rich have made Powell's dream a reality.

They systematically identify the brightest and most promising teenagers, then school them in the Austrian School of Economics.[a] Whether he was one of the boys and girls from Wichita—and I've found no evidence that he is—the path followed by Ted Cruz, a Senator from Texas seeking the Republican nomination for the Presidency, is emblematic of that trod by the Boys and Girls from Wichita.

When 13, his father signed Cruz up for classes at the Free Enterprise Institute, where he spent hundreds of hours studying the Constitution, the Federalist Papers and other founding documents. According to the *Washington Post*, Cruz was one of five teens in the institute's constitutional collaborators program, in which kids memorized the Constitution, wrote speeches and performed for Rotary clubs and other groups across Texas. "Cruz was the star," wrote the *Post*.[2]

It was a program "very much committed to private property, free markets, and constitutionally limited government," according to Winston Elliott III, who became affiliated with it when Cruz was a student and now serves as its president.[3]

THE AUSTRIAN SCHOOL OF ECONOMICS

The linchpin of the message from Charles and David Koch and their like-minded allies in the economics community or who have grown rich, is the Austrian School of Economics, especially the message of one its leading proponents, F.A. Hayek, whose book, *The Road to Serfdom*, is virtually required reading.

The website of the Mises Institute, which offers *The Road to Serfdom* for sale, describes it as "spell-binding" and "classic" that "as singularly responsible for launching an important debate on the relationship between political and economic

---

[b] (...continued)
of elections through independent expenditures should be protected with the same vigor as individual political speech. Much of the future Court opinion in *Citizens United v. Federal Election Commission* relied on the same arguments raised in *Bellotti*.

[a] Former U.S. Federal Reserve Chairman, Alan Greenspan, speaking of the originators of the Austrian School of Economics, said in 2000, "the Austrian School have reached far into the future from when most of them practiced and have had a profound and, in my judgment, probably an irreversible effect on how most mainstream economists think in this country." (See Greenspan, Alan. "Hearings before the U.S. House of Representatives' Committee on Financial Services. U.S. House of Representatives' Committee on Financial Services. Washington D.C. 25 July 2000.)

freedom."[4] Hayek, like some of his later admirers, won a Nobel Prize for Economic Sciences in 1974.[5]

It is strange that those who invoke Hayek's memory take positions that seem to differ from his. We know, for example, that those who profess adherence today to Hayek's teachings—House Speaker Paul Ryan of Wisconsin, for example, claims that his ideas are inspired by Hayek, and he even hands out copies of *The Road to Serfdom* "to bring new staffers up to speed"—pointedly disagree with Hayek.[6]

Ryan's budget calls for Medicare and Medicaid to be converted to voucher systems, and he opposes the Affordable Care Act, or Obamacare. Yet Hayek wrote that "there is no reason why … the state should not help to organize a comprehensive system of social insurance." One commentator concluded that "[Hayek] advocated mandatory universal health care and unemployment insurance, enforced, if not directly provided, by the state".[7]

Of course, we can only guess what Hayek's views would be on contemporary issues, because he died in 1992.[8] We do know, however, his views on accepting science and new theories quite well, for he told us the following:

> I find that the most objectionable feature of the conservative attitude is its propensity to reject well-substantiated new knowledge, because it dislikes some of the consequences which seem to follow from it—or, to put it bluntly, its obscurantism. I will not deny that scientists, as much as others, are given to fads and fashions, and that we have much reason to be cautious in accepting the conclusions that they draw from their latest theories.

> But the reasons for our reluctance must themselves be rational and must be kept separate from our regret that the new theories upset our cherished beliefs. I can have little patience with those who oppose, for instance, the theory of evolution or what are called mechanistic explanations of the phenomena of life because of certain moral consequences, which at first seem to follow from these theories, and still less with those who regard it as irrelevant or impious to ask certain questions at all. By refusing to face the facts, the conservative only weakens his own position.[9]

Yet Cruz and the thousands of other young men and women have become Boys and Girls from Wichita. Like *The Boys from Brazil* in Ira Levin's novel about attempts to re-create Adolph Hitler by replicating his childhood, they are cut from the same mold: very bright young men and women, captured during their youth by one or another of the Koch-Scaife-Bradley, etc. incubators, schooled in what they are told is the philosophy of Austrian school of economics and groomed for greater—perhaps, even, great—things. So far, no one has made it to the very first tier of American politics, but the second, third and fourth levels are littered with them.

During this same period the Kochs gave $30.5 million to 221 colleges and universities, often to fund academic programs advocating their world view of fewer government regulations on business and lower taxes—attitudes which happen to also be good for their petroleum-based business.[10]

All of these organizations are unknown to 99 percent of the population; and their common source of support—the rich—are unknown to most of the rest. They have provided the grist for right wing—they prefer to use the term "conservative," presumably to at once provide a convenient link to the past and to disguise what the Kochs readily admit is truly revolutionary thinking.

The Institute for Humane Studies (IHS) was relocated from California to the Arlington, Virginia campus of George Mason University, a public school. There, Charles Koch and Richard Fink had established a center for free market research and scholarship. The mission of IHS is to rear a cadre of Boys and Girls from Wichita who are unquestioning supporters of limited government and spending and the "free" market.

IHS does this by handing out scholarships starting in high school, continuing through college and beyond. Regular seminars keep students up to date on emerging issues, and they are placed as interns, not only at like-minded institutions, but with members of Congress, in the executive branch of conservative Presidents—anywhere they might be able to rise, and help the cause.

A good example of this grooming is the rise of Nancy Pfotenhauer, a girl from Wichita, created from the ground up by the Kochs. She was a graduate research assistant at George Mason University, which is the largest recipient of Koch money, to Walter Williams, who is a board member of Americans For Prosperity, in the early 1990s.

She became chief economist at the Republican National Committee (1988). She worked for George H. W. Bush's transition team (1988) and then (until 1990) for Sen. William L. Armstrong (R-CO); in 1990 she was appointed chief economist of the President's Council on Competitiveness.[11]

By the mid-1990s, Pfotenhauer was executive vice president of both Citizens for a Sound Economy and its foundation, CSEF. Later, she ran the Washington office of Koch Industries, and in 2001 joined the Independent Women's Forum, which shared a Washington address, and some of the same operational staff with Americans for Prosperity until 2008.[12]

That year, she was senior campaign advisor and spokesperson to the 2008 Republican Candidate for President, Sen. John McCain of Arizona. Today, Pfotenhauer is the president of MediaSpeak Strategies, a Washington, D.C. public relations firm, whose clients range from Fortune 100 companies to large public policy organizations and foundations. She is a member of the board of visitors at George Mason University and on the board of directors at the Cato Institute, which was founded by the Koch brothers.[13]

Another of the kids from Wichita is Matt Kibbe. In 2015, he was a Senior Advisor of Concerned American Voters, a single-candidate superPAC in support of Libertarian Kentucky Sen. Rand Paul for the 2016 Republican nomination for President. It had raised nearly $1.9 million by the end of 2015.[14]

In 2012, Kibbe was paid $469,897 by FreedomWorks and related organizations.[15] In 2010, Kibbe wrote with FreedomWorks Chairman Dick Armey, *Give Us Liberty: A Tea Party Manifesto*.[16] Kibbe was President of FreedomWorks, which is supported by the Koch brothers, from 2004 to 2015, which he joined as a policy analyst in 1986, while it was still known as Citizens for a Sound Economy, founded and supported by the Koch brothers.[17]

Kibbe later said of Citizens for a Sound Economy that its driving force was to take the Kochs' "heavy ideas and translate them for mass America. … We read the same literature Obama did about nonviolent revolutions—Saul Alinsky, Gandhi, Martin Luther King. We studied the idea of the Boston Tea Party as an example of nonviolent social change. We learned we needed boots on the ground to sell ideas, not candidates."[18]

Kibbe was Managing Editor of *Market Process*, an academic economics journal published by the Center for the Study of Market Processes (now named the Mercatus Center) at George Mason University. The Center was founded by Richard Fink at Rutgers University, but moved to George Mason in the mid-1980s after the Koch family gave it more than $30 million.[19]

FreedomWorks worked hand-in-glove with the Koch brothers-funded group, Americans for Prosperity, to help rally the Tea Party movement in 2009.[20]

Kibbe articles have appeared in the *Wall Street Journal*, the *Washington Times*, *USA Today*, RedState.com, *America Spectator,* and *Reason* magazine. On television, Kibbe has appeared on MSNBC's The Dylan Ratigan Show, MSNBC's Hardball, FOX News' Fox & Friends, FOX News' Glenn Beck, NBC's The Today Show, FOX News' America's Newsroom, C-SPAN, FOX News' Neil Cavuto, and FOX Business Network's Happy Hour.[21]

Richard Fink became another acolyte of Charles Koch. The silver-haired strategist largely unknown outside a small circle of like-minded conservative operatives, has spent more than 30 years overseeing Charles' philanthropic, political and public policy endeavors.

Fink is officially an executive vice president of Koch Industries, where he has spent much of his career overseeing the company's legal lobbying and public affairs divisions, and integrating them into a single unit that was eventually dubbed Koch Companies Public Sector.[22]

But Fink is more—much, much more. He is on the board of directors of Koch Industries Inc., Georgia-Pacific and Flint Hills Resources, LLC., and a member of the boards of directors and President of the Charles G. Koch Charitable Foundation and the Claude R. Lambe Charitable Foundation. He is also on the board of the Fred C. and Mary R. Koch Foundation.

Fink co-founded Citizens for a Sound Economy, where he served as president, and co-founded the Citizens for a Sound Economy Foundation. He also sits on the board of the Institute for Humane Studies, and the Mercatus Center at George Mason University, the Market-Based Management Institute, and Americans for Prosperity Foundation.[23]

George Mason University quickly became a magnet for those interested in the Austrian school of economics as Charles poured millions into the program. It grew into a bastion of what author Daniel Schulman has described as "an influential and feisty bastion of deregulatory policy."[24]

When the George W. Bush Administration searched for rules to repeal, the Mercatus Center nominated 14 of the 23 eventually adopted. In reporting this, the *Wall Street Journal* said the Center was wielding a "big stick".[25]

As the Mercatus Center grew, so, too, did Fink's relationship with the Kochs. Americans for Prosperity (AFP) was co-founded in 2004 by the Koch brothers and Fink, by then an executive vice president at George Mason University.[26]

Soon, the deregulatory agenda became too big for just George Mason, so Charles pumped millions of dollars into hundreds of universities. Between 2007 and 2011 alone, his giving amounted to $31 million—a pittance to one of the world's richest people—to endow professorships and sponsor conferences and lectures by libertarian advocates. They continued the support provided over the years to anti-regulatory, non-profit centers like the Cato Institute and the Mercatus Center, and expanded it to new ones.[27]

These groups began to pour out policy papers, op-eds and other arguments for profitizing government and turning it into a center friendly to free enterprise. They argued for privatizing (or, in my terms, profitizing) social security; argued that global warming was not real, or if it was, it was part of a natural cycle; converting Medicare and Medicaid into private voucher systems; and expanding the use of charter schools, to name but a few.

At the same time, they stole a chapter from Lewis Powell's Manifesto, and began mobilizing activists. They founded Citizens for a Sound Economy (CSE), claiming that it has tens of thousands of members, but in reality money came only from the Kochs and few other sources. Headed by former White House counsel C. Boyden Gray and budget director James Miller, CSE launched campaigns targeting agencies from the Justice Department (after Microsoft gave $380,000) to the Army Corps of Engineers (after sugar companies in danger of losing acreage to grow cane to a Corps Everglades restoration gave $700,000).[28]

CSE linked to the tobacco industry, arguing against increased taxes on cigarettes, teaming with Philip Morris to develop an anti-tax campaign. Then, in 1994, CSE rallied forces opposed to the Clinton Administration's plans for national health insurance, showing up at rallies with a broken-down bus, towed from stop to stop, with "This is Clinton Care" spray painted on its side.[29]

By 1997, three of the foundations controlled by the Kochs—the Charles G. Koch, David H. Koch and Claude R. Lambe foundations of Wichita, Kansas—were among a dozen that spent $79.2 million between 1992 and 1994 on think tanks and advocacy groups and $88.9 million to support scholarships and college programs to train free-market thinkers.[30]

These foundations spread the financial load, and others in that group have been leaders in supporting education. Their efforts include the Intercollegiate Studies Institute (ICI), whose alumni include Justices Antonin Scalia and Samuel Alito of the U.S. Supreme Court, author and right-wing columnist Ann Coulter, author and nationally syndicated radio host Laura Ingraham, and Edwin J. Feulner Jr., one of the founders of The Heritage Foundation.[31] ICI received in 2015, for example, grants of $430,000 from the Kirby Foundation of New Jersey, and in 2014, a grant of $390,000 from the Murdock Charitable Trust.[32]

ICI is linked to the Collegiate Network (CN), established in 1979 to provide financial and technical assistance to right-wing student newspapers on college campuses. It is heavily funded by right-wing foundations and claims its newspapers have a combined distribution of more than two million each year.[33] (See Appendix D for a list of colleges and universities with papers supported by CN.)

In addition to these over-arching programs, the Koch brothers support a number of others aimed at bringing along the Boys and Girls from Wichita. They include the following:

- **The Koch Scholars Program**: various universities provide weekly meetings, basis to discuss "an assortment of select books, movies and podcasts." Koch Scholars receive a $1,000 stipend.

- **The Koch Internship Program:** "a paid opportunity for individuals who are interested in free-market ideas and want to gain the tools to become more effective advocates for economic freedom. Interns work in substantive roles at think tanks, policy institutes, and grassroots organizations. In addition to the professional experience, interns are challenged through management training and professional education seminars each week." Interns generally work between 20 and 40 hours each week, including all day on Tuesdays. Interns are paid an hourly rate of $10.00, and receive Washington Metro or transit benefits.

This far reaching program of identifying, schooling and grooming for greater things, the Boys and Girls from Wichita, like all of the Koch brothers' efforts, is made possible only by money, an immense amount of it, far more than you or I will ever have, or dream of having. Money, and lots of it, is what oils the well-lubricated machine of neoliberalism that today threatens to end the world's greatest experiment in democracy and, with it, the United States of America.

CHAPTER 5 ENDNOTES

1. Edwin Feulner, "The Legacy of Joseph Coors," The Heritage Foundation, http://www.heritage.org/about/speeches/the-legacy-of-joseph-coors, accessed Jan. 20, 2016.

2. Marc Fisher, "Principled or Know-It-All?" *Washington Post*, March 24, 2015

3. Jeffrey Toobin, "The Absolutist," *New Yorker*, June 30, 2014.

4. Mises Institute, https://mises.org/library/road-serfdom-0, accessed Dec. 22, 2015.

5. Nobelpriz.org, prize.org/nobel_prizes/economic-sciences/laureates/1974/hayek-lecture.html, accessed Dec. 22, 2015.

6. Bernard Harcourt, "How Paul Ryan Enslaves Friedrich Hayek's The Road to Serfdom," *The Guardian*, 12 Sep. 12, 2012.

7. Nicholas Wapshott, *Keynes Hayek: The Clash That Defined Modern Economics,* Norton, W. W. & Company, Inc (2011).

8. Sylvia Nasar, "Friedrich von Hayek Dies at 92," *New York Times*, March 24, 1992.

9. F. A. Hayek , *Why I Am Not A Conservative,* The University of Chicago Press (1960).

10. Jane Mayer, "Koch Pledge Tied to Congressional Climate Inaction," *New Yorker,* June 30, 2013.

11. Wikipedia, "Nancy Pfotenhauer," https://en.wikipedia.org/wiki/Nancy_Pfotenhauer, accessed Nov. 20, 2015.

12. The Center for Media and Democracy, "Americans for Prosperity," http://www.sourcewatch.org/index.php?title=Americans_for_Prosperity#cite_ref-13, accessed Nov. 20, 2015.

13. George Mason University, http://economics.gmu.edu/programs/la-ma-econ/meet-an-alum/293, accessed Nov. 20, 2015.

14. Open Secrets.org, "Concerned American Voters," http://www.opensecrets.org/pacs/lookup2.php?strID=C00525899, accessed Dec. 17, 2015.

15. "Freedomworks 2012 Form 990" (PDF). GuideStar. Internal Revenue Service.

16. Harper Collins, New York, 2010.

17. Wikipedia, "Matt Kibbe," https://en.wikipedia.org/wiki/Matt_Kibbe#cite_note-1, accessed Dec. 17, 2015.

18. History Commons, "Profile: Matt Kibbe," http://www.historycommons.org/entity.jsp?entity=matt_kibbe_1, accessed Dec. 17, 2015.

19. Wikipedia, "Mercatus Center," https://en.wikipedia.org/wiki/Mercatus_Center, accessed Dec. 17, 2015.

20. Paul Blumenthal, "FreedomWorks, Koch Brothers Clash Over Cato Institute Takeover Bid," *Huffington Post*, April 12, 2012.

21. Wikipedia, "Matt Kibbe," https://en.wikipedia.org/wiki/Matt_Kibbe#cite_note-1, accessed Dec. 17, 2015.

22. Daniel Schulman, "Charles Koch's Brain," September/October 2014, *Politico*, http://www.politico.com/magazine/politico50/2014/charles-kochs-brain.html, accessed Dec. 22, 2015.

23. Wikipedia, "Richard Fink," https://en.wikipedia.org/wiki/Richard_Fink#Koch_Industries, accessed Dec. 22, 2015.

24. Daniel Schulman, *Sons of Wichita*, Grand Central Publishing, New York, 2014.

25. Bob Davis, "In Washington, Tiny Think Tank Wields Big Stick on Regulation With White House Ex-Staffers, Mercatus Helps Zap Codes It Says Restrict Business," *Wall Street Journal,* July 16, 2004.

26. Eric Holmberg , Alexia Fernandez Campbell," Koch: Climate pledge strategy continues to grow," July 1, 2013, Investigative Reporting Workshop, American University School of Communication, http://investigativereportingworkshop.org/investigations/the_koch_club/story/Koch_millions_spread_influence_through_nonprofits/, accessed Dec. 7, 2015.

27. Daniel Schulman, *Sons of Wichita*, Grand Central Publishing, New York, 2014.

28. Daniel Schulman, *Sons of Wichita*, Grand Central Publishing, New York, 2014.

29. Daniel Schulman, *Sons of Wichita*, Grand Central Publishing, New York, 2014.

30. Stephen Barr, "12 Foundations Push Conservative Agenda; $210 Million Given Over 3 Years," *Washington Post*, July 2, 1997.

31. Intercollegiate Studies Institute, https://home.isi.org/prominent-alumni#sthash.Y00XkNUx.dpuf, accessed Dec. 19, 2015.

32.
https://fconline.foundationcenter.org/search/results?collection=grants&activity=form&_new_search=1&grantmaker_key=&grantmaker_name=&grantmaker_location=&grantmaker_country=&grantmaker_state=&grantmaker_county=&grantmaker_city=&grantmaker_msa=&grantmaker_cd=&grantmaker_zip=&recipient_name=Intercollegiate+studies+institute&location=&recipient_country=&recipient_state=&recipient_county=&recipient_city=&recipient_msa=&recipient_cd=&recipient_zip=&recip_type=&subjects=&support_strategy=&transaction_type=&range=year_authorized&range_start=&range_stop=&keywords=&save_sort=y&sort_by=year_authorized&sort_order=1, a fee-for-service site providing information on grantors and grantees

33. http://www.rightwingwatch.org/content/collegiate-network#sthash.mfVh8Wcp.dpuf, accessed Dec. 18, 2015.

6

Consequences—And the Triumph of Neoliberalism[a]

Let's cut to the chase: Republicans support tax cuts for the rich, because that's what the rich want. And the Republicans? They just want to get elected, and contributions from the rich give them a leg up—a big leg.

The rich, however, demand more than merely tax cuts and increases in income. Just as a carpenter whose only tool is a hammer sees every problem as a nail, the rich see every threat as a potential attack on their wealth.

Those ultra-rich—roughly a third of whom have made their money directly off of fossil fuels like oil and coal and another third have made their money indirectly by investing in those same commodities—perceive threats as political, even though they are nothing of the sort.

If the rich see it that way, so do Republicans.

In their zeal to capture as much American money as possible, the rich—aided by Republicans in exchange for their financial campaign support—have cut the heart out of working America, the middle class. Today, for the first time in memory, the middle class is no longer a majority in America. The majority is now the poor and the rich, very rich and ultra-rich.

A gap between the rich and the middle class has grown inexorably, and experts say it will continue to grow. In the United States, half the 7.5 million jobs lost during the Great Recession were in industries that pay middle-class wages,

---

[a] According to Investopedia, the term "liberal" in economics is different than in politics. Liberalism in economics refers to "freeing up" the economy by removing barriers and restrictions, such as regulations or other controls on what actors can do. Neoliberalism's policies seek to create a *laissez-faire* system.

ranging from $38,000 to $68,000. But only 2 percent of the 3.5 million jobs gained since the recession ended in June 2009 are in mid-paying industries. Nearly 70 percent are in low-paying industries, and 29 percent in industries that pay well.[1]

In the process of removing the middle-class, the income and wealth gaps between the ultra-rich and everybody else has grown to a chasm.

Over the past three decades, the share of household wealth owned by the top 0.1 percent has increased from 7 percent to 22 percent. For the bottom 90 percent of families, a combination of rising debt, the collapse of the value of their assets during the financial crisis, and stagnant real wages have led to the erosion of wealth.[a, b]

In a nation in which one-tenth of one percent own 22 percent of the nation's wealth, something's wrong. Especially if that nation is the United States, founded and sustained on the notion that all are created equal.

(The disappearance of America's middle class can be graphically illustrated, as shown in an interactive graphic by the *New York Times*.[2] For Chicago alone, this shift is shown in an amazing graphic.[3])

For four decades or more, the "middle" class of America was a majority. But today its members account for only 49.9 percent of the population, down from 61 percent in 1971. Today, the poor and ultra-rich—and there is a vast gap in wealth and income between those two—are a majority.

"There's been a hollowing out in the middle, a bulking up on the edges," said Rakesh Kochhar, lead author of the recent Pew Research Center study, "The American Middle Class Is Losing Ground," told the *New York Post*. He added that the wealth of upper-income families is now about seven times that of the middle class, compared with three times about 30 years ago.[4]

---

[a] Angela Monohan, "US wealth inequality - top 0.1% worth as much as the bottom 90%," *The Guardian*, Nov. 3, 2014.

[b] Dozens of analyses have reached the same conclusion. Another, this one by the non-partisan Congressional Budget Office, found that between 1979 and 2007, the income of the top 1 percent of earners grew by a staggering 275 percent, while the bottom 20 percent gained only 18 percent. Meanwhile, the income of the next highest 19 percent of earners grew by only 60 percent, and for the middle 60 percent, income grew by approximately 40 percent. James Moreland, "Where Has the Middle Class Gone?" http://economyincrisis.org/content/where-has-the-middle-class-gone, April 8, 2014, accessed Jan. 1, 2016.

Sociologists say the middle class is composed of a series of "upper" income workers, like white-collar specialists (lawyers, engineers, professors, economists and architects); and a "middle" income of lower-level white-collar workers (teachers, nurses, insurance sales people and real estate agents). Together, these two groups make up about 45 percent of households and sit near the upper end of the income distribution, just behind the top 1 percent.[5]

At least two-thirds of adults told an ABC News poll that being middle class meant owning a home, being able to save for the future, and afford things like vacation travel, the occasional new car, and various other little luxuries.[6]

"'Middle class' in politics is not a numerical value," said Kathleen Hall Jamieson, director of the Annenberg Public Policy Center at the University of Pennsylvania. "When voters hear 'middle class,' they don't hear people who make above or below this amount of money, they hear 'us'. It's a way for politicians to signal to voters that 'I share your values.'"[7]

That seems like a good definition. It is one that I grew up with, as did most Americans. Today, if politicians are on the side of the rich—and by

ARE YOU "MIDDLE CLASS"?

The Census Bureau does not have an official definition of "middle class," so ABC News put together a list to help readers figure out whether they were:

1. You make more than $32,900 a year. A study by the Pew Charitable Trust in 2011 on the mobility of the middle class defines a family of four with two adults and two children as middle class if they make over $32,900 a year, falling between the 30th and 70th percentiles of income distribution in America.

2. You make less than $64,000 a year. The same study defines the upward limit as $64,000 a year.

3. You're likely to say you're middle class, even if you make more (or less) money than that. According to a Gallup/USA Today poll, 42 percent of Americans identify themselves as "middle class". Only 2 percent say they are "upper class", and 10 percent say they're "lower class".

4. You probably think it's hard to make ends meet. In 2012, a different report from Pew found that 87 percent of those who called themselves "middle class" say "it is more difficult now than it was a decade ago for middle-class people to maintain their standard of living."

5. Having a secure job is probably more important to you than owning a home. Another report found that unlike 21 years ago, when 70 percent of Americans thought that owning a home was the most important factor in determining if you're in the middle class, a secure job is now the most important bellwether. Second on the list? Health insurance.

6. You may not always be in the middle class. The Pew study found that growing up middle class doesn't mean you'll always be in the middle class. In fact, they found that a third of Americans raised in the middle class fall out as adults. The report found that "Marital status, education, test scores and drug use have a strong influence on whether a middle-class child loses economic ground as an adult."

Source: Andrew Springer, "6 Ways to Tell if You're Middle Class," ABC News, July 23, 2013.

virtually every measure, they are—they are no longer with "us", the middle class of America.

It means that income and wealth are unequal, and with that, so are other things. America, instead of being a nation founded on common values, a country where one President, George H.W. Bush, could be born to great wealth yet volunteer to be the youngest of all American pilots in World War II, while another—also born to great wealth and destined to become President, John Kennedy—could also volunteer to serve in the Navy and be grievously injured. Two men, both wealthy—but like all other Americans. Two men, one a Republican, the other a Democrat—but both Americans.

Today, Americans differ from one another. They are not the same. The disparity in wealth and income is vast, and growing. So is the disparity in other things.

If money is speech, as the Supreme Court has said in its *Citizens United* decision, then the rich have more speech than the rest of us, because they have more money.

If they have more money, which is manna of heaven to politicians, then they have greater influence over decisions and policies. And to create and maintain a nation that is friendly to the rich and their money, requires decisions and policies every bit as calculated and forceful as those imposed by the Soviet Union. The difference is the outcome; the process is the same.

So called "free" markets are the end product of social engineering and political will. They are unyielding. They are not a natural state of affairs, but an outcome that is just as much dictated and created as is that of planned economies. They are the product of a philosophy seldom mentioned in the United States, except by the Koch brothers, Ted Cruz and others who embrace something called "neoliberalism".[8]

Neoliberalism holds that the state is tyrannical and oppressive.[9] Why? Because that's what the rich believe.

Not all forms of capitalism are the same. There are variations in the United States, Europe, Japan and China. But by far the most virulent is that of the United States.

American capitalism, with its overriding objective of serving the interests of the rich and their property, holds that all obstacles to doing just that—regulations, controls, unions, taxes, public ownership—are unjustified and should be removed. Not so elsewhere, where these are at least tolerated and often encouraged.

Conflict over the distribution of wealth has always been at the heart of the American political process. "The genius of American politics," says Kevin Phillips, "has been to manage through ballot boxes and electoral votes the problems that less fluid societies resolve with party structures geared to class warfare and even with barricades."[10]

What the Republican Party and the rich have done is change those politics, and with it, the outcomes of these wars. Today's Republicans, almost to a person, propose to continue what they have established: a government of the rich, by the rich, and for the rich.

Trump, Bush and Rubio have each unveiled tax cut plans that would, in the words of *New York Times* columnist Paul Krugman, "lavish huge cuts on the wealthy while blowing up the deficit."[11] Of course, Krugman is an unabashed liberal but, give him credit. Krugman is also a 2008 Nobel laureate, former professor of economics at MIT, and Princeton Universities, and currently Distinguished Professor of Economics at the Graduate Center of the City University of New York.[12] He worked for Martin Feldstein when the latter was appointed chairman of the Council of Economic Advisers and chief economic advisor to President Ronald Reagan, so he's no stranger to either Washington or conservative thinking on economics.[13]

The Economist, a magazine not known for its liberalism, has said of Krugman—

> What is beyond dispute is that Mr Krugman is the finest economist to become a media superstar—at least since Milton Friedman or, earlier, John Maynard Keynes turned to journalism. Mr. Krugman's work on currency crises and international trade is widely admired by other economists.[14]

The tax plan offered by Ted Cruz, the Texas Senator, is even more simple than those of his rivals—and more radical. He would repeal both the payroll tax and the corporate tax, substituting an across the board income tax of 10 percent and a flat tax. According to the Tax Foundation, a conservative Washington-based think tank founded in 1937 (they're the ones who bring you "Tax Freedom Day" every year),[15] Cruz's plan would lose a few trillion dollars over a decade.[16]

According to James Kwak, best known as co-founder of the economics blog "The Baseline Scenario",[17] Cruz's proposal would cut taxes by $3.6 trillion over ten years, more than the U.S. plans propose to spend on the military. But in what Kwak says is an "astonishingly naked handout to the very rich", Cruz's plan would give 60 percent of the tax cut to the top 1 percent.[18]

All of these proposals would further widen the gap within inequality, and these days virtually everything in America is distributed unequally, not just income. For example, when the U.S. Supreme Court holds that campaign advertising cannot be constrained, because money is speech, then the wealthy have not only more income than the rest of us, but the right to speak more than the rest of us.

Many of the unequal results are the result of income that is not only greater for the rich, but more certain. The rest of America may or may not receive its share of the national income, but the rich and ultra-rich will. The United States has become a two-tier society, divided between rich and poor.

A Pew Research Center analysis of wealth found that the gap between America's upper-income and middle-income families has reached its highest level on record in 2013: the median wealth of the nation's upper-income families ($639,400) was nearly seven times the median wealth of middle-income families ($96,500). This was the widest wealth gap seen in 30 years since the Federal Reserve began collecting these data.

Pew's found that rich parents tend to coddle their kids, creating busy after-school schedules full of soccer games and violin lessons. Working-class kids, however, are left much more to their own devices, given fewer resources and less stroking, which makes them more independent and closer to their parents.

Yet when those children arrive at the working years, what they have inherited is the same struggle that confronted their parents.

Such inequality did not always exist in America. Changes in tax law during the Presidency of George W. Bush that reduced the federal tax rate on capital gains income is "by far the largest contributor" to rising income inequality in the United States, according to Thomas Hungerford, an economist at the Congressional Research Service (CRS). (CRS is an arm of the Library of Congress).[19]

Capital gains and other investment income—something that ordinary Americans know little about, because they work for wages in the form of a weekly check or envelope—were taxed at the same rate as regular wages until 1996, when the capital gains rate was reduced. Then, it was cut further under Bush tax cuts. That has allowed for massive income gains for the wealthy, leading directly to larger and larger income inequality.[20]

Hungerford's findings are similar to his 2011 CRS study, which found that while *income grew 25 percent from 1996 to 2006 for all Americans, it grew 74 percent for the top 1 percent and 96 percent for the top 0.1 percent. That study also found that tax cuts on capital gains, initially proposed by President George W. Bush, were the biggest driver of the disparity.*[21]

Starting with its enactment, top earners pay a higher capital gains tax rate because of a surcharge to help pay for "Obamacare," or the Affordable Care Act—something every Republican candidate for President has pledged to repeal.[22] So have all Republicans in the Senate[23] and the Republican House (more than 50 times).[24] Even with the surcharge in place, however, and capital gains rate having increased to 20 percent at the beginning of 2013, the U.S. rate remains far lower than the top income tax rate of other nations. Inequality is about the same in the United States as in Pakistan and the Ivory Coast.[25]

In a sense, Republican candidates may be reaping the harvest from the seeds they themselves have sown. They laid the foundation for their 1994 election to the House majority for the first time in 40 years by turning back efforts by President Bill Clinton to enact a tax on the energy content of fuels (to reduce causes of global warming) and to adopt health reforms. "(T)he failure to make substantive policy changes in 1993 and 1994 clearly facilitated the political changes in November 1994," a reference to Republican capture of control of the U.S. House of Representatives, the right-leaning Heritage Foundation would later report.[26]

From the outset of their modern hegemony in 1994 following the embrace of the Contract With America, the clarion call for Republicans has been to cut the budget. Time and again, they have called for less spending and fewer programs. As House Appropriations Committee chairman, Rep. Hal Rogers, R-Ky., said of proposed 2011 cuts, they would "go far and wide, and will affect every community in the nation" but are "necessary to show that we are serious about returning our nation to a sustainable financial path."[27]

What must be borne in mind is that we are not discussing just the policies proposed by Republican candidates for President, or GOP members of the House and Senate, or Republicans who are governors, or of speakers of the assembly or leaders of state senates, or attorneys general, or mayors or county executives or members of school boards. These are the policies of virtually every Republican official in the United States, and many of the voters as well.

Budget cuts trigger instability. Study after study has shown that, in the words of one group of authors, there is "a clear correlation between fiscal retrenchment and instability." Testing to see if the instability—a polite term for riots and violence in the streets—resulted from economic downturns or budget cuts, the researchers cleared depressions and recessions, concluding that "this is not the case."[28]

Study after study has reached the same conclusion: austerity leads to anarchy[a]. And "neoliberalism"—not exactly a word that rolls easily off the tongue or with which we are familiar—leads to austerity.

We are more than familiar with the philosophy of neoliberalism, however, because it was first invoked in modern times by Ronald Reagan's famous line "Government is not the solution to our problem, government is the problem."[29]

It is a philosophy embodied today by the entire Republican Party, and virtually all of the rich, which one writer has described as—

> Neoliberalism is grounded in the "free, possessive individual", with the state cast as tyrannical and oppressive. The welfare state, in particular, is the arch enemy of freedom. The state must never govern society, dictate to free individuals how to dispose of their private property, regulate a free-market economy or interfere with the God-given right to make profits and amass personal wealth. State-led "social engineering" must never prevail over corporate and private interests. It must not intervene in the "natural" mechanisms of the free market, or take as its objective the amelioration of free-market capitalism's propensity to create inequality.[30]

If this sounds familiar, it is. It is exactly what has happened—*what is happening*—in the United States. The rich are getting richer, and the poor are getting poorer.

---

[a] *South American nations:* Voth HJ. Tightening Tensions: Fiscal Policy and Civil Unrest in Eleven South American Countries, 1937–1995. Available at SSRN 2012620. 2012 Feb 28. *Queensland, Australia:* Martson G. Queensland's Budget Austerity and Its Impact on Social Welfare: Is the Cure Worse than the Disease. *J. Soc. & Soc. Welfare.* 2014;41:147. *China in the 1930s:* Braggion F, Manconi A, Zhu H. International Liquidity Shocks, the Real Economy, and Social Unrest: China, 1931–1935. *Twenty advanced economies, more than 800 general elections over 140 years:* Funke M, Schularick M, Trebesch C. Going to Extremes: Politics after Financial Crisis, 1870-2014. CESifo Working Paper; 2015.

Speaking for myself, and I suspect a good many others, I am happy to have a government that builds roads, puts out house fires, polices (admittedly unequally) the city streets, pays Social Security, provides health care whether its Medicare, Medicaid or Obamacare, cleans up after superstorms like Katrina and Sandy, rebuilds the Twin Towers, compensates those who fought the fires started by the 9/11 terrorists, adopts and enforces laws that protect people of color, drivers and other consumers, provide air and water that are safe, fights wars and shelters, however poorly, all Americans.

I do not believe government is an evil. But Republicans today do, and so do the rich and the ultra-rich.

It is not surprising, therefore, that in October 2013, as the third election after the *Citizens United* decision approached, the NBC News/Wall Street Journal poll found an electorate that was angry, in record numbers.[31]

More than six in ten Americans said it was time to give a "new person a chance" to represent them in Congress, about 11 percent more than those who agreed with that statement in October 1994, just before Republicans surged to take the House majority, when 49 percent of Americans said they wanted someone new. In 2013, just 29 percent said they felt as though their own member of Congress deserved to be reelected, a decline of 10 percent from 1994.[32]

The "give someone else a try" number had never been higher in NBC-WSJ polling. The last time the desire to try someone new had been almost as high was in the summer of 2010, just a few months before a whopping 58 Democratic incumbents lost in a massive wave election for Republicans.[33]

The result in 2014 was a massive sweep by the Republican Party, with a nine-seat gain in the U.S. Senate, 13 in the U.S. House and two Governorships.[34] The rich and Republicans had once again won. Now they were preparing for the elections of 2016.

CHAPTER 6 ENDNOTES

1. Bernard Condon and Paul Wiseman, Associated Press, "Millions Of Middle-Class Jobs Killed By Machines In Great Recession's Wake,"Jan. 23, 2013, updated March, 25, 2013, *Huffington Post*.

2. Alicia Parlapiano, Robert Gebeloff and Shan Carter, "The Shrinking American Middle Class" *New York Times*, Jan. 26, 2015. Graphic at http://www.nytimes.com/interactive/2015/01/25/upshot/shrinking-middle-class.html

3. John Dodge, "Amazing Graphic Shows Chicago's Middle Class Disappear Before Your Eyes," April 3, 2014, CBSNews, accessed Jan. 1, 2016, found at http://chicago.cbslocal.com/2014/04/03/amazing-graphic-shows-chicagos-middle-class-disappear-before-your-eyes/

4. John Aidan Byrne, "The rise and fall of the American middle class," *New York Post*, Dec. 27, 2015.

5. Hope Yen, Associated Press, "What does it mean to be 'middle class?'" *Christian Science Monitor*, July 18, 2012.

6. Hope Yen, Associated Press, "What does it mean to be 'middle class?'" *Christian Science Monitor*, July 18, 2012.

7. Hope Yen, Associated Press, "What does it mean to be 'middle class?'" *Christian Science Monitor*, July 18, 2012.

8. An approach to economics and social studies in which control of economic factors is shifted from the public sector to the private sector. Drawing upon principles of neoclassical economics, neoliberalism suggests that governments reduce deficit spending, limit subsidies, reform tax law to broaden the tax base, remove fixed exchange rates, open up markets to trade by limiting protectionism, privatize state-run businesses, allow private property and back deregulation. "Neoliberalism," Investopedia, http://www.investopedia.com/terms/n/neoliberalism.asp, accessed Jan. 6, 2016.

9. Stuart Hall, "The march of the neoliberals," *The Guardian*, Sep. 12, 2011.

10. Kevin Phillips, *The politics of rich and poor : wealth and the American electorate in the Reagan aftermath*, 1991, New York: Harper.

11. Paul Krugman, "Voodoo Never Dies," *New York Times*, Oct. 2, 2015

12. Wikipedia, "Paul Krugman," https://en.wikipedia.org/wiki/Paul_Krugman, accessed Dec. 29, 2015.

13. Wikipedia, "Paul Krugman," https://en.wikipedia.org/wiki/Paul_Krugman, accessed Dec. 29, 2015.

14. *The Economist*, "The one-handed economist; Face value." Nov. 15, 2003.

15. Kevin Drum, "Political Animal," *Washington Monthly*, Oct. 10, 2007, accessed Dec. 28, 2015.

16. Josh Barro, "Ted Cruz's Tax Plan Is Simple, Yet Radical," *New York Times*, Dec. 29, 2015.

17. Wikipedia, "James Kwak," https://en.wikipedia.org/wiki/James_Kwak, accessed Jan. 5, 2016.

18. http://baselinescenario.com/2015/11/04/60-of-ted-cruzs-tax-cut-goes-to-the-top-1/, accessed Jan. 4, 2016.

19. Travis Waldron, "Capital Gains Tax Cuts 'By Far' The Biggest Contributor To Growth In Income Inequality, Study Finds," Feb 20, 2013, ThinkProgress, http://thinkprogress.org/economy/2013/02/20/1616651/capital-gains-tax-cuts-by-far-the-big gest-contributor-to-growth-in-income-inequality-study-finds/, accessed Dec. 27, 2015.

20. Travis Waldron, "Capital Gains Tax Cuts 'By Far' The Biggest Contributor To Growth In Income Inequality, Study Finds," Feb 20, 2013, ThinkProgress, http://thinkprogress.org/economy/2013/02/20/1616651/capital-gains-tax-cuts-by-far-the-big gest-contributor-to-growth-in-income-inequality-study-finds/, accessed Dec. 27, 2015.

21. Travis Waldron, "Capital Gains Tax Cuts 'By Far' The Biggest Contributor To Growth In Income Inequality, Study Finds," Feb 20, 2013, ThinkProgress, http://thinkprogress.org/economy/2013/02/20/1616651/capital-gains-tax-cuts-by-far-the-big gest-contributor-to-growth-in-income-inequality-study-finds/, accessed Dec. 27, 2015.

22. Ballotpedia, "2016 presidential candidates on healthcare," https://ballotpedia.org/2016_presidential_candidates_on_healthcare, accessed Dec. 29, 2015. Some have said that they would "replace" ACA, which to the author is a distinction without a difference.

23. Russell Berman, "'Promise Kept': The Senate Finally Votes to Repeal Obamacare," *The Atlantic*, Dec 4, 2015.

24. Kathleen Miller and Terrence Dopp, "Core of Obamacare Would Be Repealed in Bill Passed by U.S. House," *Bloomberg Politics*, Oct. 23, 2015.

25. Travis Waldron, "Capital Gains Tax Cuts 'By Far' The Biggest Contributor To Growth In Income Inequality, Study Finds," Feb 20, 2013, ThinkProgress, http://thinkprogress.org/economy/2013/02/20/1616651/capital-gains-tax-cuts-by-far-the-big gest-contributor-to-growth-in-income-inequality-study-finds/, accessed Dec. 27, 2015.

26. Jeffrey B. Gayner, "The Contract with America: Implementing New Ideas in the U.S.," The Heritage Foundation, Oct. 12, 1995, http://www.heritage.org/research/lecture/the-contract-with-america-implementing-new-ideas -in-the-us, accessed Jan. 5, 2016.

27. Tom Curry, "What GOP budget cuts say about party priorities," NBC News, Feb. 16, 2011, http://www.nbcnews.com/id/41609293/ns/politics/t/what-gop-budget-cuts-say-about-party-priorities/#.VovQXFLMLo0, accessed Jan. 5, 2016.

28. Ponticelli J, Voth HJ. Austerity and anarchy: Budget cuts and social unrest in Europe, 1919–2008. Available at SSRN 1899287. 2011 Dec.

29. "Inaugural Address," Jan. 20, 1981, Ronald Reagan Presidential Library, http://www.reaganfoundation.org/reagan-quotes-detail.aspx?tx=2072, accessed Jan. 20, 2016.

30. Stuart Hall, "The march of the neoliberals," *The Guardian*, Sep. 12, 2011.

31. Chris Cillizza, "The mood of the American electorate? Throw MY bum out." *Washington Post*, Oct. 31, 2013

32. Chris Cillizza, "The mood of the American electorate? Throw MY bum out." *Washington Post*, Oct. 31, 2013

33. Chris Cillizza, "The mood of the American electorate? Throw MY bum out." *Washington Post*, Oct. 31, 2013

34. "Campaign 2014, CBS News, http://www.cbsnews.com/elections/2014, accessed Jan. 4, 2016.

7
CONCLUSION

There can be little doubt that the electorate in 2016 is also, like that before the 2014 elections, bitter and angry.

According to an NBC/Wall Street Journal poll, 62 percent of Americans believe the country is on the wrong track, while only 30 percent said the country is headed in the right direction. It was the 11th year running that "wrong track" beat "right track" in the NBC/WSJ data at the mid-point of the George W. Bush presidency.[1]

Fully 80 percent of Americans describe themselves as angry at a political system they see as rigged against them, anxious about the economy and their financial future, or both.[2]

Are they right? Is the political system rigged against them?

The evidence suggests that the correct answer is "yes". But that is not the response being provided by Republicans. They are, as they have since 1980, sided with the money of the rich and their own re-elections. They have, in short, stopped looking out for us, the middle class.

In truth, the culture—of Washington and that of America—started with the election of Ronald Reagan. Certainly, it was the beginning of the end of moderation in the Republican Party, a philosophy that once was found on the East and West coasts, across the Upper Midwest and in unlikely states, such as Kansas and Kentucky.

Since 1980, we have ceased to be Americans and instead are Republicans or Democrats or, increasingly, Independents. We careen from one fiscal crisis to the next—first the Savings and Loan debacle, in which roughly one-third of the nation's S&Ls failed, to the dot.com bubble's collapse, one after another of recessions, followed by the Great Recession, wars in Iraq (twice) and Afghanistan that we know of, and others of which we are ignorant.

Is this a nation that would today produce almost simultaneously John Kennedy and George H.W. Bush, both destined to become President, but of different parties—but both, above all else, Americans?

Until as recently as a decade ago, the share of total national income going to workers was relatively stable at around 70 percent, while the share going to capital—mainly corporate profits and returns on financial investments—made up the other 30 percent. Slowly but steadily, labor's share of total national income in the U.S. and many other developed countries has been falling, while the share going to capital owners has gone up. One clear result of this has been the skyrocketing wealth of the top one percent, attributable mostly to huge increases in capital gains and investment income.

During the period 2010–2012, *the top one percent are said to have received 95 percent of the growth in income and, according to a 2013 Credit Suisse report, now own 41 percent of all global assets.*[3] About 3.4 billion people—just over 70 percent of the global adult population—have wealth of less than $10,000.[4]

The ultra-rich have created a nation in which they are reaping immense— some might say obscene—profits by persuading themselves and many other Americans that "government is the enemy", in the words of Ronald Reagan. Ironically, today, that may be more true than ever, but because of the policies adopted when Reagan was President, not despite them.

As a result of the savings and loan scandals, regulators made over 30,000 criminal referrals, producing over 1,000 felony convictions.[a]

In contrast, the "Great Recession", which started under President George Bush, was about 70 times the size of the S&L scandal. It claimed about $16.4 trillion—equal to $141,501 in debt per family[b]—in U.S. household wealth from its

---

[a] Joshua Holland, "Hundreds of Wall Street Execs Went to Prison During the Last Fraud-Fueled Bank Crisis," Sep. 17, 2013, http://billmoyers.com/2013/09/17/hundreds-of-wall-street-execs-went-to-prison-during-the-last-fraud-fueled-bank-crisis/, accessed Feb. 6, 2016.

[b] "U.S. Treasury Securities," EPITrading.com, http://eiptrading.com/16-4-trillion/ accessed Feb. 6, 2016.

peak in the spring of 2007 to its bottom in the first quarter of 2009, according to figures from the Federal Reserve.[a]

After the Great Recession, the Office of Thrift Supervision made zero criminal referrals. The Office of the Comptroller of the Currency made zero criminal referrals. The Federal Reserve made three referrals for discrimination, but seems to have made zero for criminal activity, and the Federal Deposit Insurance Corporation refused to answer an inquiry, but seems to have made—you guessed it—zero criminal referrals.[b]

Zero.

That, more than anything, explains the relationship between the ultra-rich in today's America to those of us of ordinary means. The nation—you and me—lost more than the national debt. Yet those responsible paid nothing.

The ultra-rich and the Republican Party have created radical inequality, an unjust society that is driving the nation toward disaster.

From today's perspective, inequality of wealth and income—not only in the U.S. but most developed economies—has begun to look like the natural state of capitalism rather than an exception. This demonstrates that while "free" markets can create widespread prosperity, they also have the potential to create concentrations of wealth and political power. That is the case today, and the wealth and power are being used to entrench the rich and ultra-rich, whose profits owe more to favorable regulation and political connections than innovation and efficiency.[5]

The previous chapter said that of the 7.5 million jobs lost during the Great Recession, which were in industries that pay middle-class wages, only roughly about 70,000 gained have been in such mid-paying industries. Instead, almost 70 percent of the restored jobs have been in low-paying industries.[6]

In the 17 European countries that use the euro as their currency, the numbers are even worse. Almost 4.3 million low-paying jobs have been gained since

---

[a] Chris Isidore, "America's lost trillions," CNNMoney, June 9, 2011.

[b] Joshua Holland, "Hundreds of Wall Street Execs Went to Prison During the Last Fraud-Fueled Bank Crisis," Sep. 17, 2013, http://billmoyers.com/2013/09/17/hundreds-of-wall-street-execs-went-to-prison-during-the-last-fraud-fueled-bank-crisis/, accessed Feb. 6, 2016.

mid-2009, but the loss of mid-paying jobs has never stopped. Indeed, a total of 7.6 million such jobs are said to have disappeared between January 2008 and June 2013.[7]

Nobel laureate Joseph Stiglitz, the Columbia professor and former economic advisor to Bill Clinton, agrees. In his book *Rewriting the Rules of the American Economy: An Agenda for Growth and Shared Prosperity,*[8] Stiglitz provided a roadmap for policies that would reduce the inequality gap immensely.

It is not the "inexorable laws of economics" that have led to what Stiglitz calls "America's great divide," but "our policies and our politics," he writes. People tire of hearing about Scandinavian success stories, he said, "but the fact of the matter is that Sweden, Finland and Norway have all succeeded in having about as much or faster growth in per capita incomes than the United States and with far greater equality."[9]

"The American political system is overrun by money," Stiglitz writes, continuing, "Economic inequality translates into political inequality, and political inequality yields increasing economic inequality."[10]

Stiglitz offers a number of provocative insights but his key takeaway is that inequality is not inevitable. Indeed, it is largely responsible for the fact that every economic "recovery" since the 1990s has been slower and longer than the one before.[11]

Inequality isn't the trade-off for economic growth. If Stiglitz is right, it is both the cause and the symptom of slower growth.

The point here is not whether Stiglitz is right or wrong, but that the issue of income and wealth inequality is being utterly ignored by Republicans and the rich alike.

Inequality has grown in America and Europe over the last several years. The response of Republicans and most rich—the neoliberals of the Austrian School of Economics—is to insist that inequality is the price of growth.[12] That is, to continue growing we must be willing to tolerate an ever-increasing wealth gap.[13]

Moreover, the wealth gap is not to be merely tolerated, but actually pursued aggressively. If that requires ignoring the science that underpins global warming and dozens of other ills facing humanity, then so be it. They will.

We can always depend on the rich—and their allies, the Crazy, Right Wing Republicans.

CHAPTER 7 ENDNOTES

1. John King, "Polls show angry, anxious electorate for 2016, CNN Politics, Sep. 29, 2015.

2. John King, "Polls show angry, anxious electorate for 2016, CNN Politics, Sep. 29, 2015.

3. Credit Suisse, "Global Wealth Reaches New All-Time High," 2013 Credit Suisse Wealth Report, https://www.credit-suisse.com/us/en/about-us/research/research-institute/news-and-videos/articles/news-and-expertise/2013/10/en/global-wealth-reaches-new-all-time-high.html, accessed Jan . 20, 2 016. The following year, global wealth had grown to a record $263 trillion in mid-2014, $20.1 trillion more, and an 8.3 percent increase, over mid-2013.

4. Jill Treanor, "Half of world's wealth now in hands of 1% of population—report," *The Guardian*, October 13, 2015.

5. Daron Acemoglu & James Robinson, *Why Nations Fail: The Origins of Power, Prosperity, and Poverty* (Crown Publishing, 2011).

6. Drum, K. "Welcome, Robot Overlords. Please Don't Fire Us?" *Mother Jones*, 2013.

7. Bernard Condon & Paul Wiseman, "Millions Of Middle-Class Jobs Killed By Machines In Great Recession's Wake," Associated Press, 2013.

8. W W Norton & Co Inc, 2015.

9. Joseph E. Stiglitz, "Inequality Is Not Inevitable," *New York Times* blog, June 27, 2014, http://opinionator.blogs.nytimes.com/2014/06/27/inequality-is-not-inevitable/, accessed Jan. 6, 2016.

10. Joseph E. Stiglitz, "Inequality Is Not Inevitable," *New York Times* blog, June 27, 2014, http://opinionator.blogs.nytimes.com/2014/06/27/inequality-is-not-inevitable/, accessed Jan. 6, 2016.

11. Rana Foroohar, "Here's the Secret Truth About Economic Inequality in America, *Time,* May 12, 2015, accessed Jan. 6, 2016.

12. Sydney Williams, "Inequality - The Siren Call of Progressives," Austrian Economics Center, undated, http://www.austriancenter.com/2014/01/08/inequality-the-siren-call-of-progressives/, accessed Jan. 6, 2016.

13. James Pethokoukis, "Obama's inequality argument just utterly collapsed," April 11, 2012, American Enterprise Institute, http://www.aei.org/publication/obamas-inequality-argument-just-utterly-collapsed/, accessed Jan. 6, 2016. Pethokoukis does not contend that the income gap doesn't exist, but rather that it is smaller than Stigletz and others say: "median household income—properly measured—rose 36.7%, not 3.2%," according to him.

APPENDIX A
STATE POLICY NETWORK
MEMBERS AND ASSOCIATE MEMBERS

Advance Arkansas Institute
Phone: 501-588-4245
E-mail: advancearkansas@gmail.com
Web: http://www.advancearkansas.org

Alabama Policy Institute
Phone: (205) 870-9900
E-mail: taylord@alabamapolicy.org
Web: http://www.alabamapolicy.org

Alaska Policy Forum
Phone: (907) 334-5853
E-mail: info@alaskapolicyforum.org
Web: http://www.alaskapolicyforum.org

Arkansas Policy Foundation
Phone: (501) 537-0825
E-mail:
kaza@arkansaspolicyfoundation.org
Web:
http://www.arkansaspolicyfoundation.org

Beacon Center of Tennessee
Phone: (615) 383-6431
E-mail: justin@beacontn.org
Web: http://www.beacontn.org

Bluegrass Institute for Public Policy
Solutions
Phone: (270) 782-2140
E-mail: jwaters@freedomkentucky.com
Web: http://www.bipps.org

Buckeye Institute for Public Policy
Solutions
Phone: (614) 224-4422
E-mail: info@buckeyeinstitute.org
Web: http://www.buckeyeinstitute.org

Caesar Rodney Institute
Phone: (302) 734-2700
E-mail: bek@caesarrodney.org
Web: http://www.caesarrodney.org

California Public Policy Center
Phone: 714-573-2201
E-mail: contact@calpolicycenter.org
Web: http://www.calpolicycenter.org

Calvert Institute for Policy Research
Phone: (410) 752-5887
E-mail: info@calvertinstitute.org
Web: http://www.calvertinstitute.org

Cardinal Institute for West Virginia Policy
E-mail: garrett@cardinalinstitute.com
Web: http://cardinalinstitute.com/

Cascade Policy Institute
Phone: (503) 242-0900
E-mail: john@cascadepolicy.org
Web: http://www.cascadepolicy.org

Center of the American Experiment
Phone: (612) 338-3605
E-mail:
Mitch.Pearlstein@AmericanExperiment.org
Web: http://www.americanexperiment.org

Commonwealth Foundation
Phone: (717) 671-1901
E-mail:
info@commonwealthfoundation.org
Web:
http://www.commonwealthfoundation.org

Empire Center
Phone: (518) 434-3100
E-mail: thoefer@empirecenter.org
Web: http://www.empirecenter.org

Empower Mississippi Foundation
E-mail: grantcallen@gmail.com
Web: http://empowerms.org/

Ethan Allen Institute
Phone: (802) 695-1448
E-mail: eai@ethanallen.org
Web: http://www.ethanallen.org

Foundation for Government Accountability
Phone: 239-244-8808
E-mail: tbragdon@FloridaFGA.org
Web: http://www.FloridaFGA.org

Freedom Foundation (formerly Evergreen
Freedom Foundation)
Phone: (360) 956-3482
E-mail:
tmccabe@myfreedomfoundation.com
Web: http://myfreedomfoundation.com/

Freedom Foundation of Minnesota
Phone: (612) 354-2160
E-mail: annettemeeks@gmail.com
Web:
http://www.freedomfoundationofminnesota
.com

Georgia Center for Opportunity
Phone: (770) 242-0001
E-mail:
randy.hicks@georgiaopportunity.org
Web: http://www.georgiaopportunity.org/

Georgia Public Policy Foundation
Phone: (404) 256-4050
E-mail: kmccutchen@gppf.org
Web: http://www.gppf.org

Goldwater Institute
Phone: (602) 462-5000
E-mail: info@goldwaterinstitute.org
Web: http://www.goldwaterinstitute.org

Grassroot Institute of Hawaii
Phone: (808) 591-9193
E-mail: info@grassrootinstitute.org
Web: http://www.grassrootinstitute.org

Great Plains Public Policy Institute
Phone: (605) 334-9400
E-mail: ron.williamson@greatplainsppi.org
Web: http://www.greatplainsppi.org

Idaho Freedom Foundation
Phone: (208) 258-2280
E-mail: wayne@idahofreedom.net
Web: http://www.idahofreedom.org

Illinois Policy Institute
Phone: (312) 346-5700
E-mail: jtillman@illinoispolicy.org
Web: http://www.illinoispolicy.org

Independence Institute
Phone: (303) 279-6536
E-mail: jon@i2i.org
Web: http://www.i2i.org

Indiana Policy Review Foundation
Phone: (260) 417-4094
E-mail: cladwig@inpolicy.org
Web: http://www.inpolicy.org

James Madison Institute
Phone: (850) 386-3131
E-mail: bob@jamesmadison.org
Web: http://www.jamesmadison.org

John Locke Foundation
Phone: (919) 828-3876
E-mail: kswanson@johnlocke.org
Web: http://www.johnlocke.org

John William Pope Civitas Institute
Phone: (919) 834-2099
E-mail: Francis.DeLuca@nccivitas.org
Web: http://www.nccivitas.org/

Josiah Bartlett Center for Public Policy
Phone: (603) 224-4450
E-mail: arlinghaus@jbartlett.org
Web: http://www.jbartlett.org

Kansas Policy Institute
Phone: (316) 634-0218
E-mail: dave.trabert@kansaspolicy.org
Web: http://www.kansaspolicy.org

Libertas Institute
E-mail: info@libertas.org
Web: http://www.libertasutah.org

MacIver Institute for Public Policy
Phone: (608) 588-6477
E-mail: bhealy@maciverinstitute.com
Web: http://maciverinstitute.com/

Mackinac Center for Public Policy
Phone: (989) 631-0900
E-mail: lehman@mackinac.org
Web: http://www.mackinac.org

Maine Heritage Policy Center
Phone: (207) 321-2550
E-mail: mgagnon@mainepolicy.org
Web: http://www.mainepolicy.org

Maryland Public Policy Institute
Phone: (240) 686-3510
E-mail: csummers@mdpolicy.org
Web: http://www.mdpolicy.org

Mississippi Center for Public Policy
Phone: (601) 969-1300
E-mail: thigpen@mspolicy.org
Web: http://www.mspolicy.org

Montana Policy Institute
Phone: (406) 219-0508
E-mail: brent.mead@gmail.com
Web: http://www.montanapolicy.org

Nevada Policy Research Institute
Phone: (702) 222-0642
E-mail: am@npri.org
Web: http://www.npri.org

New Hampshire Center for Economic
Policy
E-mail: akreins@gmail.com
Web: http://www.nheconomics.org

Oklahoma Council of Public Affairs
Phone: (405) 602-1667
E-mail: Michael@ocpathink.org
Web: http://www.ocpathink.org

Pacific Research Institute
Phone: (415) 989-0833
E-mail: spipes@pacificresearch.org
Web: http://www.pacificresearch.org

Palmetto Promise Institute
Phone: (803) 708-0673
E-mail: Ellen@palmettopolicy.org
Web: http://www.palmettopolicy.org/

Pelican Institute for Public Policy
Phone: (504) 267-9404
E-mail: kkane@pelicaninstitute.org
Web: http://www.pelicaninstitute.org/

Pioneer Institute
Phone: (617) 723-2277
E-mail: jstergios@pioneerinstitute.org
Web: http://www.pioneerinstitute.org

Platte Institute for Economic Research
Phone: (402) 452-3737
E-mail: jvokal@platteinstitute.org
Web: http://www.platteinstitute.org

Public Interest Institute
Phone: (319) 385-3462
E-mail: racheter@limitedgovernment.org
Web: http://www.limitedgovernment.org

Public Policy Foundation of West Virginia
Phone: (304) 282-8249
E-mail: jfshaffer@comcast.net

Rhode Island Center for Freedom and
Prosperity
E-mail: info@rifreedom.org
Web: http://rifreedom.org

Rio Grande Foundation
Phone: (505) 264-6090
E-mail: pgessing@riograndefoundation.org
Web: http://www.riograndefoundation.org

Show-Me Institute
Phone: (314) 454-0647
E-mail:
brenda.talent@showmeinstitute.org
Web: http://www.showmeinstitute.org

South Carolina Policy Council
Phone: (803) 779-5022
E-mail: eal@scpolicycouncil.com
Web: http://www.scpolicycouncil.com

Sutherland Institute
Phone: (801) 355-1272
E-mail: si@sutherlandinstitute.org
Web: http://www.sutherlandinstitute.org

Texas Public Policy Foundation
Phone: (512) 472-2700
E-mail: brollins@texaspolicy.com
Web: http://www.texaspolicy.com

Thomas Jefferson Institute
Phone: (703) 440-9447
E-mail: mikethompson@erols.com
Web: http://www.thomasjeffersoninst.org

Virginia Institute for Public Policy
Phone: (703) 753-5900
E-mail: Jtaylor@virginiainstitute.org
Web: http://www.virginiainstitute.org

Washington Policy Center
Phone: (206) 937-9691
E-mail:
dmeadsmith@washingtonpolicy.org
Web: http://www.washingtonpolicy.org

Wisconsin Policy Research Institute
Phone: (262) 367-9940
E-mail: wpri@wpri.org
Web: http://www.wpri.org

Wyoming Liberty Group
Phone: (307) 632-7020
E-mail: susan.gore@wyliberty.org
Web: http://www.wyliberty.org

Wyoming Policy Institute
Phone: (307) 286-3411
E-mail: janie@wyomingpolicy.org
Web: http://www.wyomingpolicy.org/

Yankee Institute for Public Policy
Phone: (860) 282-0722
E-mail: carol@yankeeinstitute.org
Web: http://www.yankeeinstitute.org

SPN Associate Members

1851 Center for Constitutional Law
Accuracy In Media
Acton Institute
Advocates for Self-Government
Allegheny Institute for Public Policy
Alliance for School Choice
America's Future Foundation
American Consumer Institute
American Council of Trustees and Alumni
American Enterprise Institute
American Legislative Exchange Council
American Majority
American Principles Project
American Tradition Institute
American Transparency - OpenTheBooks
Americans for Prosperity Foundation
Americans For Tax Reform
Ashbrook Center
Atlantic Legal Foundation
Atlas Network
Ayn Rand Institute
Bastiat Society[1]
Bastiat Society of Charleston
Bastiat Society of Charlotte
Bastiat Society of Cleveland
Bastiat Society of Colorado Springs
Bastiat Society of Delaware
Bastiat Society of Indianapolis
Bastiat Society of Nashville
Bastiat Society of Portland
Bastiat Society of Sacramento
Bastiat Society of San Jose
Bastiat Society of St. Louis
Bastiat Society of Wichita
Bastiat Society of Wilmington
Beacon Hill Institute
Benjamin Rush Institute
Better Government Project
Capital Research Center
Cato Institute
Centennial Institute
Center for Competitive Politics

Center for Education Reform
Choice Media
Citizens Against Government Waste
Citizens Council for Health Freedom
Claremont Institute
Compact for America Educational
Foundation
Competitive Enterprise Institute
David Horowitz Freedom Center
DonorsTrust
Education Action Group Foundation
Families Against Mandatory Minimums
Foundation for Economic Education
Foundation for Education Reform &
    Accountability
Foundation for Excellence in Education
Foundation for Self-Government
Franklin Center for Government and
    Public Integrity
Fraser Institute
Free State Foundation
Free to Choose Network
FreedomWorks
Friedman Foundation for Educational
Choice
Frontier Lab
Fund for American Studies
Galen Institute Inc.
Headspring Group
Heartland Institute
Heritage Foundation
Independent Institute
Independent Women's Forum
Institute for Humane Studies at George
    Mason University
Institute for Justice
Institute for Policy Innovation
Institute for Truth in Accounting
Intellectual Takeout
Intercollegiate Studies Institute
Jesse Helms Center

John William Pope Center for Higher
  Education
Judicial Watch Inc.
Just Facts
Keystone Community of Hope
Leadership Institute
Leadership Program of the Rockies
Liberty Foundation of America
Limited Government Forum
Louisiana Family Forum
Lucy Burns Institute
Manhattan Institute for Policy Research
Mercatus Center at George Mason
University
Moving Picture Institute
National Center for Policy Analysis
National Center for Public Policy Research
National Legal and Policy Center
National Review Institute
National Right to Work Legal Defense
  Foundation
National Taxpayers Union
National Taxpayers Union Foundation
New Jersey Family Policy Council
North Carolina Institute for Constitutional
  Law

Oregon Capitol Watch Foundation
Pacific Legal Foundation
Prometheus Institute
Property & Environment Research Center
R Street Institute
Reason Foundation
Regular Folks United
Sam Adams Alliance
Small Business Hawaii
South Carolinians for Responsible
  Government
Spark Freedom
State Budget Solutions
Steamboat Institute
Students For Liberty
Taliesin Nexus
Tax Foundation
The Liberty Foundation of America
Thomas B. Fordham Foundation
Tuerck Foundation for the Study of
  Economics, Law and the Humanities
Utah Taxpayers Foundation
Wisconsin Institute for Law & Liberty, Inc.
Young America's Foundation
Youth Entrepreneurs

OTHER ORGANIZATIONS

ACCF Center for Policy Research
Accuracy in Academia
Adams Report
Alliance Defense Fund
Alliance for Choice in Education
Alliance for Maine's Future
America's Future
American Association of Small Property
    Owners
American Center for Law and Justice
American Conservative Union
American Council on Science & Health
American Dream Coalition
American Institute for Full Employment
American Land Rights Association
American Majority
Americans for Fair Taxation
Americans for Free Choice in Medicine
Americans for Limited Government
    Foundation
Americans for Prosperity - Arizona
Americans for Prosperity - Colorado
Americans for Prosperity - Georgia
Americans for Prosperity - Illinois
Americans for Prosperity - Michigan
Americans for Prosperity - Missouri
Americans for Prosperity - NC
Americans for Prosperity - NJ
Americans for Prosperity - North Dakota
Americans for Prosperity - Oklahoma
Americans for Prosperity - South Carolina
Americans for Prosperity - South Dakota
Americans for Prosperity - Texas
Americans for Prosperity - Topeka, Kansas
Americans for Prosperity - Virginia
Americans for Prosperity - Wichita,
Kansas
Americans for Prosperity- Wisconsin
Americans United for Life
Association of American Educators
Association of American Educators
Bill of Rights Institute

Black Alliance for Educational Options
Broad Foundation
Building Excellent Schools
California Common Sense
CalWatchDog
Center for Civic Renewal
Center for Individual Freedom
Center for Self-Government in the West
Center for Union Facts
Charles G. Koch Charitable Foundation
Christian Coalition of Alabama
Citizen Outreach Foundation
Citizens Alliance of Pennsylvania
Citizens Equal Rights Alliance
Citizens for Limited Taxation
Civitas Institute
Clare Boothe Luce Policy Institute
Club for Growth
Concerned Women for America
Congressional Institute
Consumers for Health Care Choices
Cornerstone Policy Research
DCI Group Inc.
Eagle Forum
Education Advancement Fund
International
Education Liberty Watch
Ethics and Public Policy Center
Excellent Education for Everyone
Family Action Council of Tennessee
Family Research Council
Federalist Society
Florida TaxWatch
Foundation for Free Enterprise
Foundation for Individual Rights in
Education
Foundation for Research on Economics &
    the Environment
Freedom Works - California
Freedom Works - Colorado
Freedom Works - Florida
Freedom Works - Michigan

Freedom Works - North Carolina
Freedom Works - Oklahoma
Freedom Works - Oregon
Freedom Works - Texas
Freedom Works - Washington State
Freedom Works - Wisconsin
Future of Freedom Foundation
Houston Property Rights Association
Indiana Family Institute
Innosight Institute
Institute for Health Freedom
Institute of the North
Iowa Taxpayer Association
John Jay Institute
Justice Foundation
Kansas Taxpayers Network
Landmark Legal Foundation
Let Freedom Ring
Lexington Institute
Liberty Fund
Liberty Institute
Liberty on the Rocks
Lincoln Institute of Public Opinion
    Research, Inc.
Lincoln Legal Foundation
MacIver Institute for Public Policy
Maryland Taxpayers Association Inc.
Michigan Association of Public School
    Academies (MAPSA)
Montana Taxpayers Association
Mountain States Legal Foundation
National Institute for Labor Relations
    Research
National Tax Limitation Committee
National Taxpayers United-Illinois
Nebraska Tax Research Council
Nebraska Taxpayers for Freedom
Nevada Taxpayers Association
Open Government Institute of California
Oregonians in Action
Parents In Charge Foundation
Pennsylvania Leadership Conference

Performance Institute
Philanthropy Roundtable
Property Rights Foundation of America
    Inc.
Public Policy Institute of New York
Public Service Research Foundation
REACH
Religious Freedom Coalition
Research Institute for Hawaii
Rocky Mountain Foundation
Sagamore Institute for Policy Research
San Diego Institute for Policy Research
Searle Freedom Trust
Southeastern Legal Foundation
State Policy Network
State Policy Network and Institute for
    Humane Studies
State Policy Network and Institute for
    Humane Studies
Students in Free Enterprise
Susan B. Anthony List
Tax Foundation of Hawaii
Taxpayer Association of Oregon
Taxpayer's Federation of Illinois
Taxpayers Network Incorporated
Teach NYS
Tennessee for Tax Reform
Tennessee Tax Revolt
Tennessee Taxpayers Association
Texans for Fiscal Responsibility
The Atlas Society
The Center for Vision & Values at Grove
    City College
The Clemson Institute for the Study of
    Capitalism
Victims of the Endangered Species Act
    (VESA)
We the People Foundation
Wisconsin Taxpayers Alliance
Wyoming Heritage Foundation
Young America's Foundation - California

APPENDIX A ENDNOTE

1. The Bastiat Society, says that "the world is getting better, and everyone benefits when peaceful and profitable trade is allowed to thrive."

APPENDIX B
AMERICA'S RICHEST FAMILIES

Rank	Family Name	Net Worth	# Family Members	Source	Headquarters
#1	Walton	$149 B	6	Wal-Mart	Bentonville, AR
#2	Koch	$86 B	4	diversified	Wichita, KS
#3	Mars	$80 B	3	candy	McLean, VA
#4	Cargill-MacMillan	$45 B	23 (est.)	Cargill Inc.	Minneapolis, MN
#5	Cox	$34.5 B	3	media	Atlanta, GA
#6	Hearst	$32 B	66	Hearst Corp.	New York, NY
#7	Pritzker	$30 B	13	hotels, investments	Chicago, IL
#8	S.C. Johnson	$28.8 B	11	cleaning products	Racine, WI
#9	(Edward) Johnson	$26 B	4	money management	Boston, MA
#10	Duncan	$22.4 B	4	pipelines	Houston, TX
#11	Newhouse	$18 B	2	magazines, newspapers	New York, NY
#12	Lauder	$16.5 B	6	Estee Lauder	New York, NY
#13	Ziff	$15 B	3	publishing	New York, NY
#14	Du Pont	$14.5 B	3,500 (est.)	DuPont	Wilmington, DE
#15	Hunt	$14.2 B	33	oil	Dallas, TX
#16	Sackler	$14 B	20 (est.)	pain medicines	Stamford, CT
#17	Dorrance	$13.6	11 (est.)	Campbell Soup Co.	Camden, NJ
#18	Busch	$13.5 B	30 (est.)	Anheuser-Busch	St. Louis, MO
#19	(Charles & Rupert) Johnson	$13.4 B	5	mutual funds	San Mateo, CA
#20	Brown	$12.8 B	25 (est.)	liquor	Louisville, KY
#21	Mellon	$11.5	200 (est.)	banking	Pittsburgh, PA
#22	(Don & Doris) Fisher	$11 B	4 (est.)	The Gap	San Francisco, CA
#22	Rockefeller	$11 B	200 (est.)	oil	New York, NY

Rank	Family Name	Net Worth	# Family Members	Source	Headquarters
#24	Butt	$10.4 B	5	supermarkets	San Antonio, TX
#25	Gallo	$10.3 B	14 (est.)	wine, liquor	Modesto, CA
#26	Marshall	$9 B	3	diversified	Dallas, TX
#27	Crown	$8.8 B	3 (est.)	investments	Wilmette, IL
#28	Reyes	$8.6 B	3	food & beer distribution	Chicago, IL
#29	Bass	$8.2 B	4	oil, investments	Fort Worth, TX
#30	Shoen	$8 B	13 (est.)	U-Haul	Phoenix, AZ
#31	Hughes	$7.9 B	3	Public Storage Inc.	Glendale, CA
#31	Meijer	$7.9 B	4	supermarkets	Grand Rapids, MI
#31	Stryker	$7.9 B	3	inheritance	Kalamazoo, MI
#34	Pigott	$7.7 B	30	trucks	Bellevue, WA
#34	Simon	$7.7 B	5	shopping malls	Indianapolis, IN
#36	Simplot	$7.5 B	3 (est.)	agribusiness	Boise, ID
#37	Rollins	$7.4 B	11	Orkin pest control	Atlanta, GA
#38	Bechtel	$7.3 B	4 (est.)	construction, engineering	San Francisco, CA
#39	Chao	$7.2 B	3	Chemicals	Houston, TX
#39	E.W. Scripps	$7.2 B	50 (est.)	newspapers	Cincinnati, OH
#41	Cathy	$7 B	2	Chick-fil-A	Atlanta, GA
#42	Marriott	$6.9 B	7 (est.)	hotels	Bethesda, MD
#43	Jenkins	$6.8 B	25	Publix Super Markets	Lakeland, FL
#44	LeFrak	$6.6 B	4 (est.)	LeFrak Group	New York, NY
#44	Phipps	$6.6 B	300 (est.)	Carnegie Steel, Bessemer Trust	New York, NY
#46	Johnson	$6.3 B	60 (est.)	Johnson & Johnson	New Brunswick, NJ

Rank	Family Name	Net Worth	# Family Members	Source	Headquarters
#46	Smith	$6.3 B	60 (est.)	tools, banking	Chicago, IL
#48	Barbey	$6.1 B	12 (est.)	textiles, apparel	Greensboro, NC
#49	Haslam	$6 B	4	truck stops, Cleveland Browns	Knoxville, TN
#49	Kluge	$6 B	5 (est.)	TV stations, investments	New York, NY
#49	Tisch	$6 B	5	diversified	New York, NY
#49	Van Andel	$6 B	4 (est.)	Amway	Ada, MI
#53	France	$5.7 B	20	Nascar racing	Daytona Beach, FL
#54	Dolan	$5.5 B	19 (est.)	cable television	Town of Oyster Bay, NY
#54	Moran	$5.5 B	10 (est.)	Toyota distribution	Deerfield Beach, FL
#56	Getty	$5.4 B	28	Getty Oil	--
#56	Perot	$5.4 B	2	investments	Dallas, TX
#56	Simmons	$5.4 B	3	finance	Dallas, TX
#59	Durst	$5.2 B	33	real estate	New York, NY
#59	Gore	$5.2 B	24 (est.)	Gore-Tex	Newark, DE
#61	Rudin	$5.1 B	30 (est.)	real estate	New York, NY
#62	Alfond	$4.8 B	4 (est.)	shoes	Portland, ME
#63	Glazer	$4.7 B	21	real estate, sports teams	--
#63	Ingram	$4.7 B	5	book distribution, transportation	Nashville, TN
#65	McCaw	$4.6 B	5	telecom	Hunts Point, WA
#66	Ricketts	$4.5 B	6	TD Ameritrade	Omaha, NE
#67	Milliken	$4.4 B	35 (est.)	textiles	Spartanburg, SC
#67	Wirtz	$4.4 B	11	alcohol distribution	Chicago, IL

Rank	Family Name	Net Worth	# Family Members	Source	Headquarters
#69	Chandler	$4.2 B	200 (est.)	newspapers	Los Angeles, CA
#70	Friedkin	$4.1 B	2	Toyota distributor	Houston, TX
#71	Coors	$4 B	250 (est.)	beer	Golden, CO
#71	Wegman	$4 B	2 (est.)	supermarkets	Rochester, NY
#73	Hascotes	$3.9 B	8 (est.)	convenience stores	Framingham, MA
#73	Stephens (Warren, Witt & Elizabeth)	$3.9 B	3	investments	Little Rock, AR
#75	Nordstrom	$3.8 B	11	department stores	Seattle, WA
#75	Pohlad	$3.8 B	20 (est.)	real estate, banking, sports	Minneapolis, MN
#75	Steinbrenner	$3.8 B	5	New York Yankees	New York, NY
#78	Haas	$3.7 B	255 (est.)	Levi Strauss & Co.	San Francisco, CA
#79	Van Tuyl	$3.5 B	8 (est.)	car dealerships	Phoenix, AZ
#80	Gund	$3.4 B	15 (est.)	Sanka, banking	Cleveland origin, OH
#80	Lerner family	$3.4 B	3 (est.)	banking, sports teams	--
#80	(Richard Alan) Smith	$3.4 B	10 (est.)	investments	Chestnut Hill, MA
#83	Demoulas	$3.3 B	9	supermarkets	Tewksbury, MA
#83	Schneider	$3.3 B	6 (est.)	trucking	Green Bay, WI
#83	Tyson	$3.3 B	10 (est.)	Tyson Foods	Springdale, AR
#86	Karfunkel	$3.2 B	5 (est.)	insurance, real estate	New York, NY
#86	Kerkorian	$3.2 B	5	casinos, movie production	--
#86	Perdue	$3.2 B	4 (est.)	chicken	Salisbury, MD
#86	Ueltschi	$3.2 B	20 (est.)	pilot training	Flushing, NY
#90	Fertitta	$3.1 B	2	casinos, entertainment	Las Vegas, NV

Rank	Family Name	Net Worth	# Family Members	Source	Headquarters
#90	Gottwald	#3.1 B	7 (est.)	Ethyl Corp.	Richmond, VA
#90	Milstein	$3.1 B	6 (est.)	real estate	New York, NY
#93	Bresky	$3 B	3 (est.)	agribusiness	Chestnut Hill, MA
#93	Fasken	$3 B	4	oil	Midland, TX
#95	Bancroft	$2.9 B	30 (est.)	Dow Jones & Co.	New York, NY
#96	Boyle	$2.8 B	3	Columbia Sportswear	Portland, OR
#96	(Otto) Haas	$2.8 B	38	chemicals	Philadelphia, PA
#96	Hall	$2.8 B	3	Hallmark	Kansas City, MO
#96	Ziegler	$2.8 B	6 (est.)	cigars	Darien, CT
#100	Batten	$2.7 B	3 (est.)	media	Hampton Roads, VA
#100	Booth	$2.7 B	30 (est.)	investments	Los Angeles, CA
#100	Schottenstein	$2.7 B	200 (est.)	retail	Columbus, OH
#103	Asplundh	$2.6 B	130 (est.)	tree trimming	Willow Grove, PA
#103	Dobson	$2.6 B	3	Whataburger	San Antonio, TX
#103	Epprecht	$2.6 B	5 (est.)	cheese	Hiram, OH
#103	Jones	$2.6 B	7	bakery supplies	Jackson, MI
#103	Wanek	$2.6 B	2	furniture	Arcadia, WI
#103	Whittier	$2.6 B	70 (est.)	oil	Beverly Hills, CA
#109	De Young	$2.5 B	24 (est.)	newspaper, TV stations	San Francisco, CA
#109	Gochman	$2.5 B	3 (est.)	sporting goods retailer	Katy, TX
#109	Holding	$2.5 B	4	oil, resorts	Salt Lake City, UT
#109	Magness	$2.5 B	4 (est.)	cable TV, investments	Denver, CO
#109	McGraw	$2.5 B	11 (est.)	McGraw-Hill	New York, NY

Rank	Family Name	Net Worth	# Family Members	Source	Headquarters
#109	Shea	$2.5 B	20 (est.)	real estate, venture capital	Los Angeles, CA
#109	Yates	$2.5 B	16	oil	Artesia, NM
#116	Gates	$2.4 B	3	investments	Denver, CO
#116	Jackson	$2.4 B	7 (est.)	winemaking, vineyards	Sonoma, CA
#116	Wasserstein	$2.4 B	9	investment banking	New York, NY
#119	Collier	$2.3 B	30 (est.)	real estate	Naples, FL
#119	Hewlett	$2.3 B	17	Hewlett-Packard	Palo Alto, CA
#119	Mosing	$2.3 B	11 (est.)	oilfield services	Amsterdam
#122	Blaustein	#2.2 B	30 (est.)	Amoco oil	Baltimore, MD
#122	Carlson	$2.2 B	9	hotels, restaurants, travel	Minnetonka, MN
#122	Elghanayan	$2.2 B	8 (est.)	real estate	New York, NY
#122	Soffer	$2.2 B	8	real estate	--
#126	(John) Anderson	$2.1 B	5 (est.)	beer distribution, real estate	Los Angeles, CA
#126	Annenberg	$2.1 B	15 (est.)	publishing	Los Angeles, CA
#126	Walsh	$2.1 B	2	construction	Chicago, IL
#129	Belk	$2 B	20 (est.)	department stores	Charlotte, NC
#129	Farmer	$2 B	15	uniforms	Cincinnati, OH
#129	Ford	$2 B	40 (est.)	Ford Motor	Dearborn, MI
#129	Lindner	$2 B	7 (est.)	investments, insurance	Cincinnati, OH
#129	Young	$2 B	11	plastic packaging	Plymouth, MI
#134	Bean	$1.9 B	25 (est.)	L.L. Bean	Freeport, ME
#134	Bucksbaum	$1.9 B	12 (est.)	real estate	Chicago, IL
#134	Hess	$1.9 B	19	oil and gas	New York, NY

Rank	Family Name	Net Worth	# Family Members	Source	Headquarters
#134	Sheetz	$1.9 B	35 (est.)	convenience stores	Altoona, PA
#134	Trinchero	$1.9 B	4	wine	--
#139	Graham	$1.8 B	5 (est.)	Washington Post Co.	Washington, DC
#139	Krehbiel	$1.8 B	3	Electronics	Lake Forest, IL
#139	Maines	$1.8 B	2	food distribution	Conklin, NY
#139	Merage	$1.8 B	5	microwavable snacks	Englewood, CO
#139	Mitchell	$1.8 B	11 (est.)	oil	The Woodlands, TX
#139	Resnick	$1.8 B	18 (est.)	real estate	New York, NY
#139	Roberts	$1.8 B	5	cable TV	--
#139	Sorenson	$1.8 B	8	medical equipment	Salt Lake City, UT
#139	Walter	$1.8 B	2 (est.)	oil & gas	Houston, TX
#139	Yoh	$1.8 B	3	construction	Philadelphia, PA
#149	Colson	$1.7 B	3 (est.)	senior housing	Vancouver, WA
#149	Davidson	$1.7 B	10	glassmaking	Auburn Hills, MI
#149	Mark Davis	$1.7 B	7 (est.)	dairy	Le Sueur, MN
#149	Estes	$1.7 B	7 (est.)	trucking	Richmond, VA
#149	Pitcairn	$1.7 B	200	PPG Industries	Bryn Athyn, PA
#149	Reed	$1.7 B	4 (est.)	lumber, paper, land	Seattle, WA
#149	Rogers	$1.7 B	2 (est.)	Mary Kay cosmetics	Addition, TX
#149	Weyerhaeuser	$1.7 B	250 (est.)	timber	Federal Way, WA
#157	Clark	$1.6 B	4	construction, real estate	Bethesda, MD
#157	Dayton	$1.6 B	92	Target	Minneapolis, MN
#157	Donnelley	$1.6 B	10 (est.)	printing, business services	Chicago, IL

Rank	Family Name	Net Worth	# Family Members	Source	Headquarters
#157	Fisher	$1.6 B	4 (est.)	real estate	New York, NY
#157	Kim	$1.6 B	10 (est.)	semiconductor packaging	Chandler, AZ
#157	Pulitzer	$1.6 B	50 (est.)	publishing	St. Louis, MO
#163	Cullen	$1.5 B	50 (est.)	oil, coal	Houston, TX
#163	Frank	$1.5 B	3	Grey Goose vodka	New Rochelle, NY
#163	Greenberg	$1.5 B	7	sneakers	Manhattan Beach, CA
#163	(J. Erskine) Love	$1.5 B	6 (est.)	packaging	--
#163	McKee	$1.5 B	5	snack maker	Collegedale, TN
#163	Mead	$1.5 B	35	paper	Wisconsin Rapids, WI
#163	Morse	$1.5 B	5 (est.)	real estate development	The Villages, FL
#163	Searle	$1.5 B	4 (est.)	pharmaceuticals	Chicago, IL
#163	Slawson	$1.5 B	3	oil & gas	Wichita, KS
#163	Stayer	$1.5	9	sausage production	Sheboygan Falls, WI
#163	Tracy	$1.5 B	73 (est.)	food distribution	Mt. Sterling, IL
#174	Cohen	$1.4 B	5 (est.)	grocery distributor	Keene, NH
#174	Levine	$1.4 B	4 (est.)	Family Dollar	Charlotte, NC
#174	Lewis	$1.4 B	5 (est.)	insurance	Mayfield Village, OH
#174	Richards	$1.4 B	5	cable manufacturing	Carrollton, GA
#174	Westerman	$1.4 B	7	oil	Addison, TX
#179	Bolch	$1.3 B	7	convenience stores	Atlanta, GA
#179	Briscoe	$1.3 B	8 (est.)	ranch land	Uvalde, TX
#179	Cadieux	$1.3 B	4 (est.)	convenience stores	Tulsa, OK
#179	Foster	$1.3 B	5 (est.)	poultry production	Livingston, CA

Rank	Family Name	Net Worth	# Family Members	Source	Headquarters
#179	Hagedorn	$1.3 B	6	Scotts Miracle-Gro	Marysville, OH
#179	Huber	$1.3 B	40 (est.)	engineered materials	Rumson, NJ
#179	McCaskey	$1.3 B	12 (est.)	Chicago Bears	Chicago, IL
#179	(Les) Schwab	$1.3 B	4 (est.)	tire retailers	--
#179	Shorenstein	$1.3 B	3	real estate	San Francisco, CA
#179	Stewart	$1.3 B	3	food service	Scottsdale, AZ
#179	Toll	$1.3 B	2	homebuilding	Horsham, PA
#179	Wood	$1.3 B	196	Wawa convenience stores	Media, PA
#191	Hixon	$1.25 B	100 (est.)	electronics	Pasadena, CA
#191	Rosen	$1.25 B	5 (est.)	meat processing	Fairmont, MN
#193	Carhartt	$1.2 B	2	work clothing	Dearborn, MI
#193	Colburn	$1.2 B	4 (est.)	electric equipment distributor	Irving, TX
#193	(Ellen) Gordon	$1.2 B	5	Tootsie Rolls	Chicago, IL
#193	Kennedy	$1.2 B	30	investments	New York, NY
#193	Lykes	$1.2 B	250 (est.)	land, citrus groves	Tampa, FL
#193	Marciano	$1.2 B	4	Guess jeans	Los Angeles, CA
#193	Rooney	$1.2 B	15 (est.)	Pittsburgh Steelers	Pittsburgh, PA
#193	Ward family	$1.2 B	2 (est.)	chocolate	Kansas City, MO

Source: Forbes, http://www.forbes.com/families/

Appendix C
Those Thanked by the Kochs for Donating $1 Million or More to Campaigns

Those cited for having given $1 million or more at a 2011 seminar,[1] included the following:

JOHN CHILDS

Childs is the founder and CEO of private equity firm JW Childs Associates, reportedly worth $1.2 billion.

THE CORTOPASSIS

Dean "Dino" Cortopassi and his wife, Joan, are from Stockton, California. A self-made man, he founded the San Tomo Group—which counts among its enterprises Modesto-based Stanislaus Food Products, the world's largest fresh-pack tomato cannery and market leader in tomato products for Italian restaurants and pizzerias.[2]

JOE CRAFT

Joseph Craft is president, CEO, and chairman of Alliance Resource Partners, a coal company based in Tulsa, Oklahoma. His family is reportedly worth $1.9 billion.

THE DEVOSES

Rich and Helen DeVos hail from Michigan. The cofounder of Amway and owner of the NBA's Orlando Magic, Rich DeVos is reportedly worth in the ballpark of $4.2 billion. The Richard and Helen DeVos Foundation funds conservative Christian groups, such as Focus on the Family.

THE FARMERS

Dick Farmer, from Ohio, inherited his father's rag-cleaning business, and turned it into the Cintas Corporation.

THE FULLINWIDERS

Jerry Fullinwider of Dallas, Texas is vice chairman of Hillwood International Energy, which has oil operations in Iraq and Jordan as well as the United States and Russia.

THE GILLIAMS

Richard Gilliam founded the Cumberland Resources Corporation, which was one of the nation's largest private coal mining companies when Massey Energy bought it for nearly $1 billion in March 2010.

THE GRIFFINS

Ken and Anne Dias Griffin are a hedge fund power couple from Chicago, who wed in 2003. Ken is the founder and CEO of Citadel, and is reportedly worth $2.3 billion. Anne founded one of the nation's largest woman-run hedge funds, Aragon Global Management.

THE HAWORTHS

Richard Haworth is the former CEO and chairman emeritus of Haworth, an international office-interiors manufacturer based in Holland, Michigan, which he inherited in 1975, with sales of $1.4 billion in 2005, the year he retired.

DIANE HENDRICKS

Hendricks, former head of the ABC Supply roofing company, which she took over from her husband Kenneth after he died in a construction site accident in 2007, is reportedly worth $2.2 billion.

THE HUMPHREYS FAMILY

Ethelmae Humphreys, chairs the board of Tamko Building Products, a maker of asphalt shingles, of which her son, David, is CEO. They have numerous connections to the Kochs.

THE ROBERTSONS

Corbin Robertson is CEO and chairman of the board of Natural Resource Partners, a Houston-based owner of coal mines in Appalachia, the Illinois Basin, and the Western United States.

TOM RASTIN

Rastin shares a Mount Vernon, Ohio, address with Karen Wright, and is vice president of marketing and engineering at the Ariel Corporation.

APPENDIX C ENDNOTES

1. Gavin Aronsen, "Exclusive: The Koch Brothers' Million-Dollar Donor Club," *Mother Jones*, Sep. 6, 2011.

2. Joe Goldeen, "Well-wishers surprise Cortopassi," Dec. 10, 2005, http://www.recordnet.com/apps/pbcs.dll/article?AID=/20051210/MONEY/512100313/1014/NEWS10, accessed Dec. 26, 2015.

APPENDIX D
SOME COLLEGIATE NETWORK MEMBER PUBLICATIONS

The Anteater Review, University of California, Irvine

The Anthem, Texas A&M University

Areté, Berry College

The Binghamton Review, Binghamton University

The Broadside Magazine, North Carolina State University

The Brown Spectator, Brown University

The Bruin Standard, University of California, Los Angeles

California Patriot, University of California, Berkeley

California Review, University of California, San Diego

The Cardinal Principle, Stanford University

The Carolina Review, University of North Carolina

The Carrollton Record, Johns Hopkins University

The Centurion, Rutgers University

The Claremont Independent, Claremont McKenna College, Pomona College, Scripps College, Harvey Mudd College, and Pitzer College

Contumacy, University of Texas at Austin

The Cornell Review, Cornell University

The Counterweight, Bucknell University

The Counterweight, University of Minnesota-Morris

Counterpoint, University of Chicago

The Cross Examiner, Seton Hall Law School

The Dartmouth Review, Dartmouth College

The Davidson Reader, Davidson College

The Eastern Republic, Eastern Washington University

The Fenwick Review, College of the Holy Cross

The Filibuster, New York University

The Georgetown Academy, Georgetown University

The Georgetown Federalist, Georgetown University

The Georgia GuardDawg, University of Georgia

The Gonzaga Witness, Gonzaga University

The Good Bull, Texas A&M University

The Gothic Guardian, Duke University

The GW Patriot, George Washington University

The Harvard Ichthus, Harvard University

The Harvard Salient, Harvard University

The Hillsdale Forum, Hillsdale College

The Indiana Standard, Indiana University Bloomington

The Irish Rover, University of Notre Dame

The Kenyon Observer, Kenyon College

The Lehigh Patriot, Lehigh University

The Liberty, Oregon State University

Liberty Bell, Seton Hall University

Light & Truth, Yale University

Lincoln Park Statesman, DePaul University

The Michigan Review, University of Michigan

The Midway Review, University of Chicago

The Minuteman, University of Massachusetts Amherst

The Mountaineer Jeffersonian, West Virginia University

The Northwestern Chronicle, Northwestern University

The Observer at Boston College, Boston College

The Orange & Blue Observer, University of Illinois

The Oregon Commentator, University of Oregon

The Phoenix, Wabash College
Portland Spectrum, Portland State University
The Praetorian, University of California, Riverside
The Primary Source, Tufts University
Princeton Tory, Princeton University
The Purdue Review, Purdue University
The Rambler, Christendom College
The Spectator, Washington and Lee University
The Statesman, University of Pennsylvania
The Stanford Review, Stanford University
The Terrapin Times, University of Maryland
Texas Review of Law and Politics, University of Texas at Austin

The Tiger Town Observer, Clemson University
Utraque Unum, Georgetown University
The Vanderbilt Torch, Vanderbilt University
The Villanova Times, Villanova University
The Virginia Advocate, University of Virginia
The Virginia Informer, College of William & Mary
The Wabash Commentary, Wabash College
The Warrior, Marquette University
The Washington Witness, Washington University
The Yale Free Press, Yale University

APPENDIX E
Colleges and Universities with Programs
Supported by the Charles Koch Foundation
October 2015

Albany State University
Allegheny College
Alma College
American University
Amherst College
Andrew College
Appalachian State University
Arizona Christian University
Arizona State University
Ashland University
Augustana University
Austin Peay State University
Ave Maria University
Azusa Pacific University
Baldwin-Wallace University
Ball State University
Barton College
Baylor University
Beloit College
Benedictine College
Berry College
Bethel College - Indiana
Biola University
Birmingham-Southern College
Boise State University
Bowling Green State University
Brown University
Bryan College
Buena Vista University
California State University - Chico
California State University - East Bay
California State University - Fresno
California State University - Northridge
California State University - San
    Bernardino
Carroll College
Carthage College
Catholic University of America

Cedarville University
Central Connecticut State University
Central Michigan University
Chapman University
Charleston Southern University
Chestnut Hill College
Christopher Newport University
Claflin University
Claremont Graduate University
Claremont McKenna College
Clemson University
Coastal Carolina University
Colgate University
College of Charleston
College of Coastal Georgia
College of New Jersey
College of Saint Rose
College of the Sequoias
College of William and Mary
Columbia University
Corban University
Cornell University
Creighton University
Dartmouth College
Duke University
Duquesne University
East Carolina University
Eastern Florida State College
Eastern University
Elizabethtown College
Emory University
Emporia State University
Eureka College
Fayetteville State University
Florida Atlantic University
Florida Gulf Coast University
Florida Southern College
Florida State University

George Fox University
George Mason University
George Washington University
Georgetown University
Georgia College and State University
Georgia Gwinnett College
Georgia State University
Grossmont College
Grove City College
Gustavus Adolphus College
Hampden-Sydney College
Hampton University
Harvard University
Hawaii Pacific University
High Point University
Hillsdale College
Hofstra University
Hollins University
Hope College
Houghton College
Houston Baptist University
Illinois State University
Indiana University
Indiana University-Purdue University - Indianapolis
Iowa State University
Jacksonville State University
Jacksonville University
James Madison University
John Brown University
Johns Hopkins University
Johnson and Wales University
Judson University
Kansas State University
Kennesaw State University
Kenyon College
La Sierra University
Lake Forest College
Lakeland College
Lebanon Valley College
Lee University
Liberty University
Lindenwood University
Lipscomb University

Long Island University
Loyola University - New Orleans
Malone University
Manhattanville College
Massachusetts Institute of Technology
McGill University
McKendree University
Mercer University
Methodist University
Metropolitan State University of Denver
Michigan State University
Middle Tennessee State University
Millikin University
Mississippi State University
Montana State University - Bozeman
Mount Holyoke College
Mount St. Mary's University
Murray State University
New York University
Newman University
Nicholls State University
North Carolina State University
North Dakota State University
North Park University
Northern Illinois University
Northwest Nazarene University
Northwestern College - Iowa
Northwestern Oklahoma State University
Northwestern University
Oglethorpe University
Ohio Christian University
Ohio State University
Ohio University
Oklahoma State University
Patrick Henry College
Pennsylvania State University
Pennsylvania State University - Harrisburg
Pepperdine University
Presbyterian College
Providence College
Purdue University
Radford University
Ramapo College
Regent University

Rensselaer Polytechnic Institute
Roanoke College
Robert Morris University
Rochester Institute of Technology
Rockford University
Rogers State University
Rose-Hulman Institute of Technology
Rutgers University
Saginaw Valley State University
Saint Francis University
Saint Vincent College
Salisbury University
Sam Houston State University
Samford University
San Diego State University
San Jose State University
Sarah Lawrence College
Seattle Pacific University
Seton Hall University
Shasta College
Southern Illinois University
Southern Illinois University - Carbondale
Southern Methodist University
Southern University at New Orleans
Southern Virginia University
St. Ambrose University
St. Bonaventure University
St. Cloud State University
St. Edwards University
St. John Fisher College
St. John's University
St. Lawrence University
St. Mary's College of Maryland
Stanford University
State University of New York - Oswego
State University of New York - Plattsburgh
State University of New York - Purchase
Stephen F. Austin State University
Stonehill College
Suffolk University
Susquehanna University
Syracuse University
Texas A&M University
Texas State University - San Marcos

Texas Tech University
The King's College
Towson University
Transylvania University
Trinity College
Trinity University
Troy University
Tuskegee University
University of Akron
University of Alabama
University of Arizona
University of Arkansas
University of Arkansas - Little Rock
University of California - Irvine
University of Central Arkansas
University of Chicago
University of Colorado - Colorado Springs
University of Connecticut
University of Dallas
University of Dayton
University of Georgia
University of Houston
University of Illinois - Chicago
University of Kansas
University of Kentucky
University of Louisville
University of Maine - Orono
University of Mary Hardin-Baylor
University of Maryland - Baltimore County
University of Maryland - College Park
University of Michigan
University of Minnesota - Duluth
University of Missouri - Columbia
University of Nebraska - Omaha
University of Nevada - Las Vegas
University of Nevada - Reno
University of New Orleans
University of North Carolina - Greensboro
University of North Carolina at Chapel
    Hill
University of North Carolina at Pembroke
University of North Texas
University of Notre Dame
University of Oklahoma

University of Pennsylvania
University of Pittsburgh
University of Richmond
University of San Diego
University of South Alabama
University of South Florida
University of St. Thomas
University of Tampa
University of Tennessee - Knoxville
University of Texas - Arlington
University of Texas - Austin
University of Texas - Pan American
University of Tulsa
University of Virginia
University of Virginia's College at Wise
University of Washington
University of Washington - Bothell
University of West Florida
University of Wisconsin - La Crosse
University of Wisconsin - Madison
Ursinus College
Utah State University

Villanova University
Virginia Military Institute
Virginia Tech
Wake Forest University
Walden University
Washington College
Waynesburg University
Webber International University
Wellesley College
Wesleyan College
West Liberty University
West Texas A&M University
West Virginia University
Western Carolina University
Western Kentucky University
Western Michigan University
Wichita State University
Wingate University
Winston-Salem State University
Winthrop University
Wofford College
Yale University

*Funding for Kansas schools is provided by the Fred and Mary Koch Foundation.

www.ingramcontent.com/pod-product-compliance
Lightning Source LLC
Chambersburg PA
CBHW081356280526
45788CB00009B/2903